The
IRISH FIDDLE
BOOK

The Art of Traditional Fiddle-Playing

by Matt Cranitch

OSSIAN

Published by
Ossian Publications
8/9 Frith Street, London W1D 3JB, UK

Exclusive Distributors:
Music Sales Limited
Distribution Centre, Newmarket Road,
Bury St Edmunds, Suffolk IP33 3YB, UK
Music Sales Corporation
257 Park Avenue South, New York, NY1000
United States Of America
Music Sales Pty Limited
120 Rothschild Avenue,
Rosebery, NSW 2018, Australia

Design & continuity by John Loesberg
Drawings & diagrams by the author
Music engraving by Seton Music, Bantry
Cover photograph by Anna O'Connor

www.musicsales.com

Contents

For LIZ

Preface

Since the first edition of this book was published in 1988, Irish traditional music has reached new levels of popularity, with more people than before playing this music. It is to be heard not only at sessions at home in Ireland but also on concert platforms throughout the world. The amount of people who are attending weekly classes in traditional music has increased, as has the number of workshops and summer schools dedicated to various aspects of the music. Also, the study of traditional music is included on the curriculum of a growing number of third-level institutions. The fiddle continues to play a central role in these developments.

In preparing this edition of the book, consideration was given to all aspects of its contents, particularly in the context of the on-going changes taking place. The discography was revised significantly to take account of the large number of commercial recordings issued in recent years, and the bibliography has been up-dated. With regard to the central core of the book – the art of traditional fiddle-playing – it was felt that the fundamentals have not changed, and so this aspect of the book remains largely as it was, however with some minor modifications made to the text. Additional information is given on the various styles of fiddle-playing, and a demonstration CD is included.

As before, this book explains and shows in detail the various techniques used by fiddle-players in creating a traditional style of playing. It is aimed not only at the beginner, but also the fiddle-player (and indeed violinist) with some knowledge and experience who wishes to learn more. Those who once played, perhaps as children and not since, can start again: there are no age barriers to playing the fiddle! All that is necessary is a desire to play music in the traditional style.

The first chapter is an introduction to Irish traditional music, and to the fiddle itself. Chapter 2, on the fundamentals of music notation, may be omitted by those who already read music. The next two chapters, specifically for beginners, deal with holding the instrument, tuning, and playing simple melodies, some of which are well known. Starting with Chapter 5, the various techniques used by traditional fiddle-players are introduced in the context of the music itself. Individual chapters, all containing detailed musical transcriptions, are devoted to the different types of tune. Special emphasis is given to rhythm and bowing. 'Ornamentation' and 'variation' are presented gradually throughout the book. The final chapter embraces all that has been learned up to then, and more. It includes a number of tunes in which bowing and ornamentation have not been indicated, thus encouraging you to 'try it yourself'. Also the essential features of the different regional styles of fiddle-playing are outlined. Appendix A, containing 101 tunes, gives further opportunity to practise technique, develop your playing, and increase repertoire. The bibliography in Appendix B lists a number of collections and publications in which more tunes and additional information can be obtained. The discography in Appendix C provides information on an extensive range of recorded fiddle music.

The demonstration CD features a large selection of the transcribed tunes and ornaments. The symbol ( ), with the appropriate number, is used throughout the text to refer to the particular track on the recording: for example, track 2 features The Connachtman's Rambles, as on page 49. In order to demonstrate the particular points being made in each case, the examples are generally played slower than normal. On tracks 7, 8, 25 and 26, they are played at two tempos, slowly first and then faster. On each of tracks 20 and 35, two tunes are played together to comprise a set of tunes as would usually be done by traditional musicians. This CD is an invaluable aid to learning, because you can hear how the music and ornamentation should sound. Furthermore, playing along with the recording will help with rhythm and intonation, thereby increasing confidence in your own playing.

How long will it take to get through all this? That depends on whether you are a beginner or an 'improver'. It also depends on the rate of progress, and this varies from one individual to another. In all cases, it is best to work gradually through the book, learning and absorbing each point as it is made, before going on to the next section. In this way you will begin to memorise the tunes more easily, and more quickly develop a traditional style of playing: you experience a sense of satisfaction at each stage of achievement. It will take time to become an accomplished fiddle-player, but it is well worth the effort. Enjoy it!

This book could not have been written without a great deal of help and encouragement from many people. In particular, I wish to thank John Loesberg, Ossian Publications, who first suggested that I write the book, and waited patiently for so long to receive the completed manuscript. I am very grateful to Gerry O'Connor of Dundalk for his helpful advice and guidance, particularly at the earlier stages of writing, to Jackie Small for making many valuable suggestions, and helping with the titles of tunes, and to Tomás Ó Canainn, who reviewed the manuscript. For supplying photographs, information and tunes, sincere thanks are due to Julia Clifford, Mícheál Cranitch, Mick Duggan, Colin 'Hammy' Hamilton, Dave Hennessy, Dónal Hickey, Tony Kearns, The Kelly Family of Cooraclare, Caoimhín Mac Aoidh, Mrs. Julia Mary Murphy, Mick O'Connor, Joe O'Donovan, Johnny O'Leary, Muiris O Rócháin and Jack Power. I am also deeply indebted to the many fiddle-players who, unknown to themselves, were 'under observation' at sessions and concerts for a number of years – this in an effort to discover what it is that fiddle-players actually do when playing. Finally, thanks are due to Finbar Boyle, Nicholas Carolan, Tom Sherlock and Frances Hamilton for assistance in preparing the discography, to Mary O'Shea for typing the original manuscript, and to Paul Millard for photography.

1. Introduction

The fiddle has, for many years, been the instrument most widely used in the playing of Irish traditional music. It is not native, being in fact a normal violin: however, the style of playing is distinctly Irish. The melodic shape of a large number of tunes has been influenced greatly by the fiddle. This is hardly surprising, when one realizes that traditional music is composed on the instrument itself, and passed on to other musicians aurally ('by ear'), without recourse to pen and paper. The tunes are being varied continuously as they pass from one player to another, and from instrument to instrument. In essence, this makes all traditional musicians part composers as well, although they would not so regard themselves. The large collection of tunes we have today is, to a great extent, the product of generations of anonymous but gifted musicians, many of whom were fiddle-players.

While it is difficult to define exactly what Irish Traditional Music is, some of its characteristic features are well known. Many will be familiar with the instruments used, how they sound, and with musical forms such as Jigs, Reels, Hornpipes and Airs. The music is played 'by ear', and passed on from one generation to the next, as we have already seen. And what of the vitality, exuberance and beauty of the music itself?

Like any other kind of music, Irish Traditional Music has its own unique idioms, both melodic and rhythmic. These are what make it different, and are the means by which it can be recognized and interpreted. It is necessary to become familiar with them by listening to as much music as possible on records, radio programmes, and better still, 'live' at sessions and concerts. In a sense, music can be considered a language, which can only be learnt aurally.

Even though dance music accounts for the greater part of the traditional repertoire, relatively little music is actually played for dancing nowadays, being played mostly in a listening environment. Without the guidance, and indeed constraints, of the dance and dancer, the TEMPO (or speed) at which a tune is played can vary substantially from one musician to another, and from region to region. It is impossible to be definite in specifying a fixed tempo for each type of tune. The best advice is to listen and be guided by what those who are more experienced do.

The titles of dance tunes are merely names, or labels, by which they are known and identified. They usually have no musical significance, and may contain either personal or place names, because of their association with a particular musician or with some geographic region, for example **Pádraig O'Keeffe's Slide** and **The Roscommon Reel**. Others tune-titles, such as **Bonaparte's Retreat**, relate to historical events. Economic plight is evident in **I Have No Money**, while further aspects of life are reflected in **The Girl Who Broke My Heart** and **The New Potatoes**. Many tunes have several names, varying from one part of the country to another.

Of its nature, a book like this cannot hope to cover all aspects of the various styles of playing, nor can it deal exclusively with any particular one. By STYLE is meant either the way in which one musician plays, as distinct from another, or alternatively, the distinguishing features of playing which identify musicians from a particular area. It is in the latter sense that the terms 'Clare style' or 'Sligo style' are used. The differences and boundaries between the various regional styles of playing are now less obvious than before, because of the influence of recordings, radio and television. These have made music in all styles readily available to everyone, so that a particular style is no longer confined to its own region. One result of this is the emergence of individual or personal styles of playing, where aspects of different regional styles are evident. These points will be discussed in more detail later.

The fiddle, or violin, which first appeared towards the middle of the sixteenth century, has remained virtually unchanged for the past three hundred years. The shape of the body, as well as the positioning of the bridge and sound-post, contribute significantly to creating the unique tone of the instrument.
The sound-post is a wooden dowel wedged between the top and back plates. It is located under the foot of the bridge beneath the E-string. Under the other foot, a long strip of wood, known as the bass-bar, is glued to the inner surface of the top plate.

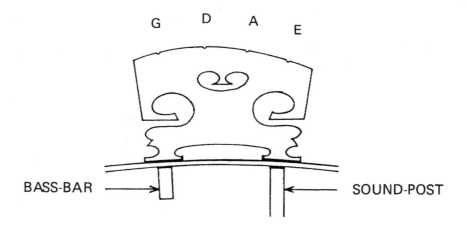

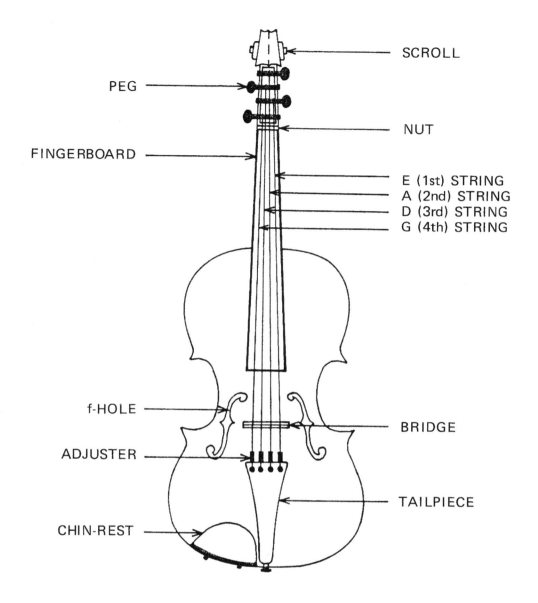

SCROLL

PEG

NUT

FINGERBOARD

E (1st) STRING
A (2nd) STRING
D (3rd) STRING
G (4th) STRING

f-HOLE

BRIDGE

ADJUSTER

TAILPIECE

CHIN-REST

The height of the strings over the fingerboard (sometimes called the ACTION), and the curvature of the bridge, are matters of personal preference. Experience will indicate if adjustments need to be made so that the instrument is comfortable to play. Any alterations and repairs which may be necessary are generally best carried-out by a violin repairer, who will also be able to give advice on the condition, age and value of instruments.

As for strings, a certain amount of trial-and-error may be necessary in selecting those, which best suit the instrument and player. Traditional musicians have a preference for steel strings, for which adjusters (also called fine tuners) are necessary in order to tune accurately. These are attached to the tailpiece.

In some ways, the bow can be thought of as being the 'other half' of the fiddle. It greatly affects tone quality, and is of course the means by which the music is made. The choice of bow is a personal matter. Some prefer a heavy bow, while others favour a light one. There is no doubt that a good bow, well balanced and easy to play with, improves the music significantly.

The ability to recognize and select a suitable bow comes with experience. Rosin should be applied to the bow regularly, to ensure that it makes good contact with the strings. When not in use, it should be 'loosened' by means of the screw at the nut (also called the frog). Repairs and re-hairing should be carried-out by an instrument repairer.

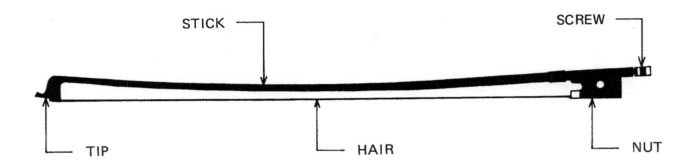

The fiddle, strings and bow-stick should be wiped clean periodically, to help prolong the life of the instrument, and maintain its tonal qualities.

2. *Music Notation*

Musical sounds are indicated by symbols called NOTES which are written on and between the five lines of the STAFF.

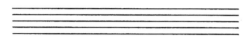

The notes are named after the first seven letters of the alphabet A, B, C, D, E, F and G. The position of a note on the staff indicates its PITCH. The higher a note is placed on the staff the higher it sounds, and the lower a note is placed the lower it sounds. In the case of music written for the fiddle, and indeed for other instruments playing traditional music, the TREBLE CLEF is used. This is indicated by a sign at the beginning of each staff.

When notes above and below the staff are required, small lines called LEGER LINES are added.

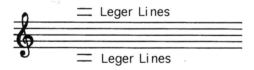

The notes placed on the five lines are E, G, B, D and F.

It may help you to memorize these if you remember that
   'EVERY GOOD BOY DESERVES FOOD'.

The notes in the spaces are F, A, C and E.

You should have little difficulty remembering these because you see them every time you look in the mirror!

Putting the lines and spaces together we get

Notice that the notes are placed alternately on lines and spaces. As we go from left to right, each note is higher on the staff than the previous note, and also sounds higher.

If we now add the leger lines, we have the following NOTE-CHART.

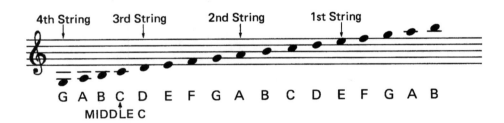

Middle C is so-called because it is the C which is located in the centre of a piano keyboard.

An INTERVAL is the musical distance between two notes. For example, starting at G as note one, B is the third note away, giving the interval of a THIRD between G and B. C to C is an OCTAVE (or an eighth). Of particular interest to the fiddle-player is the interval of a FIFTH, because the strings are tuned in fifths – G, D, A and E. The SEMITONE (Half-Tone) is the smallest interval occurring in written music: E to F and B to C are semitones. One TONE (Whole-Tone) consists of two semitones, and examples are D to E and A to B.

As well as learning to read music, you should also try to write it.
Get a manuscript book and practise making the treble clef sign.
Memorize the names of the five lines (E, G, B, D, F) and four spaces
(F, A, C, E), and learn to mark the notes in their correct places on the staff.

Some exercises will help. Try to do them without the aid of this book, and
then check against the note chart on page 12. Alternatively, get your teacher,
if you have one, to correct the exercises, and give you some more.

Copy the following notes onto your manuscript, and write the names beneath
each note.

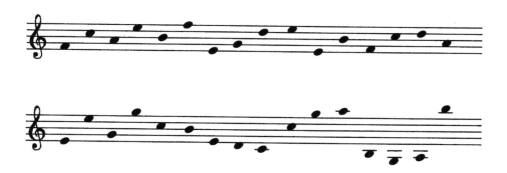

Mark, in the correct places, the following notes;-

LINES ONLY

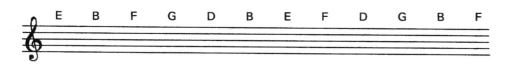

E   B   F   G   D   B   E   F   D   G   B   F

SPACES ONLY

F   C   A   E   F   A   E   F   C   E   A   C

Write the notes a THIRD above the notes given – the first is done.

Write the notes a FIFTH below the notes given – again the first is done.

There are five principal NOTE-VALUES, which are written and named as follows;-

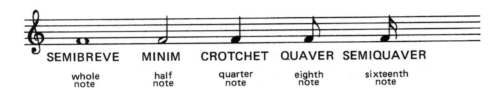

The stems of the minim, crotchet, quaver and semi-quaver are on the right-hand side of the note and upward when the note is below the middle line (B), and on the left-hand side and downward when the note is above the middle line, as in the following examples.

The note B on the middle line may have the stem upward or downward.

Quavers and semiquavers are generally joined in groups of two, three or four.

The longest note, the semibreve is twice as long as the minim; the minim is twice as long as the quaver; and the quaver is twice as long as the semiquaver.

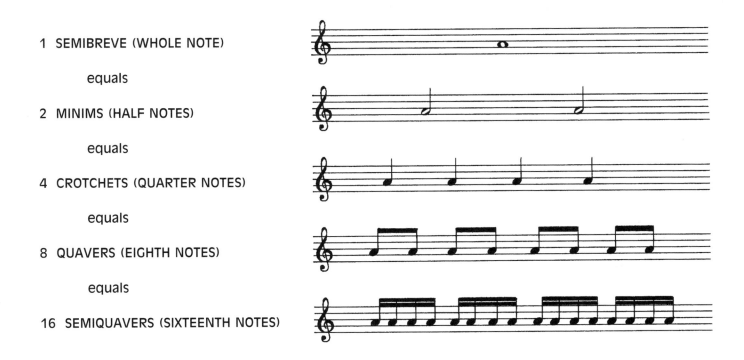

1 SEMIBREVE (WHOLE NOTE)

equals

2 MINIMS (HALF NOTES)

equals

4 CROTCHETS (QUARTER NOTES)

equals

8 QUAVERS (EIGHTH NOTES)

equals

16 SEMIQUAVERS (SIXTEENTH NOTES)

A TIE is a symbol placed over or under two notes on the same line or space to indicate that the sound is sustained for the duration of the two notes. Even though two notes are written, they sound as one.

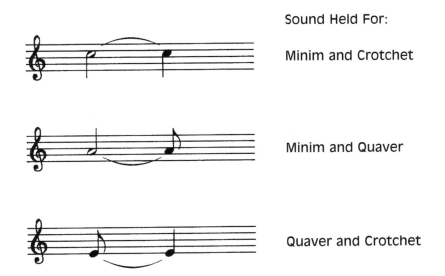

Sound Held For:

Minim and Crotchet

Minim and Quaver

Quaver and Crotchet

A DOTTED-NOTE (when a dot is placed after the note) has its duration increased by half the original value. For example, a dotted crotchet is equal to a crotchet and quaver.

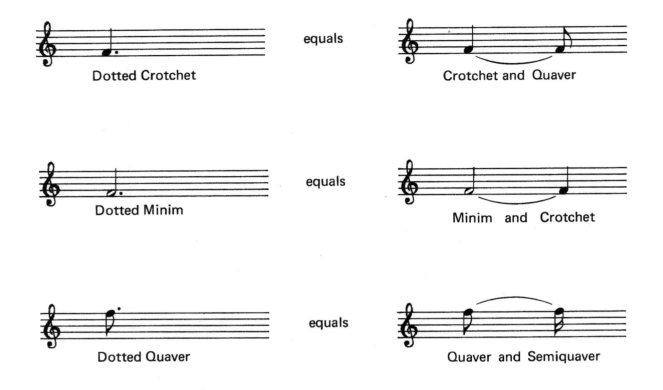

Dotted Crotchet   equals   Crotchet and Quaver

Dotted Minim   equals   Minim and Crotchet

Dotted Quaver   equals   Quaver and Semiquaver

A REST is a symbol which indicates a silence or rest in the music.
Each note value has a corresponding rest which is of the same duration.

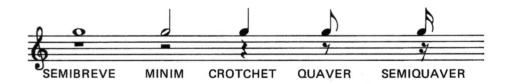

SEMIBREVE   MINIM   CROTCHET   QUAVER   SEMIQUAVER

The semibreve rest always hangs from the fourth line, and the minim rest
sits on the third line.

In your manuscript book, practise making the different kinds of notes and
rests. Write out the note-chart (page 12) using each of the note values in turn.

Music is generally written in BARS (or MEASURES) of equal duration.
These are separated by BAR-LINES drawn across the staff.
A DOUBLE BAR-LINE indicates the end of a piece, or a section within a piece.

In this example, there are four crotchets in each bar (or measure), thus making the bars equal in length.

A double-bar line with two dots placed before it indicates a REPEAT. This means returning to the previous double bar-line or, if there is none, to the beginning, to play that part of the piece again.

In this case, all five bars are repeated, whereas, in the following example, bars 3 to 6 are repeated.

The TIME-SIGNATURE, which appears at the beginning of a piece, is an indication of the METRE of the music. It tells how many BEATS there are in the bar and the duration of each beat. For example, a time-signature of $\frac{3}{4}$ indicates that there are three equal beats in every bar and that each beat is a crotchet (quarter note).

In each time-signature, the lower figure denotes the type of note, and the upper figure the number of beats.

3 – NUMBER OF BEATS
4 – CROTCHET (Quarter-Note) BEATS

The time-signature of $\frac{4}{4}$, which means four crotchet beats in each bar, is also known as COMMON TIME, and is frequently indicated by the symbol $\mathbf{C}$.

equals

We have already seen that two quavers equal one crotchet, and two crotchets equal one minim, and so on. Combinations of the various note values can go together to make up four crotchet beats in the bar.

| 1 | 2 | 3 | 4 | 1 | 2 | 3 | 4 | 1 | 2 | 3 | 4 | 1 | 2 | 3 | 4 |

As well as telling the number and type of beats in the bar, the time-signature also indicates the RHYTHM of the music. For instance, waltzes are written in $\frac{3}{4}$, while marches are in $\frac{4}{4}$. This is also the time-signature used for reels and hornpipes, and so is of particular interest.

At this stage, some counting and clapping exercises will help. Count aloud each beat, and clap each note (but not rests). Remember that the counting (1, 2, 3, 4, 1, 2, etc.) must always keep in time and not get faster or slower. Listen to the steady 'tick-tock' of a clock to get the idea. Don't forget that rests are as important as notes.

If you are having difficulty, it is helpful to count for two or three bars before you start clapping.

When counting quavers, it is usual to count as follows;-

1　　2 and 3　　4 and

Normally, this is written as 1, 2 +, 3, 4 +, where + means 'AND'.
Like the tick-tock of the clock, the count of 1, 2, 3, 4 does not change,
even when you include 'AND'.

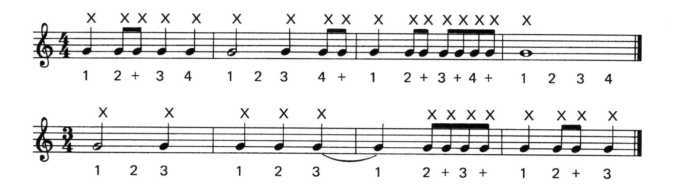

Recall that tied notes are held for the duration of the two individual notes.

Some more exercises, but this time not marked. If you wish, pencil-in the
marks and then count – better still, if you can do it without marking.

When counting a dotted note, remember that the length is increased by half
the original value.

Note that in the last exercise, the first bar is incomplete and has only one beat (beat 4): because of this, the last bar has only three beats.

Here are some more exercises, this time unmarked.

A time-signature of $\frac{6}{8}$ indicates that in each bar there are six quavers (eighth-notes), in groups of three.

As before, we can have combinations of different notes, as long as there are six quavers, in groups of three or their equivalent, in each bar.

In the case of $\frac{9}{8}$ and $\frac{12}{8}$, the quavers are also grouped in threes.

Try the following exercise.

It is more usual however to count two beats in each bar, on the first and fourth quavers – in other words, a beat for each group of three quavers. So that, the last exercise would now be

Similarly, there are three beats in the bar for $\frac{9}{8}$.

There are four beats in the bar for $\frac{12}{8}$.

When counting the following unmarked exercises, you may find it helpful at first, to count the full number of quavers in each bar. After some practice, this will no longer be necessary.

A SHARP sign (♯), placed before a note, raises it one semitone, and a FLAT sign (♭) lowers it one semitone. A NATURAL sign (♮) restores a note, already flat or sharp, to its natural position.

C SHARP   C NATURAL   B FLAT   B NATURAL

When sharps or flats are placed at the beginning of the staff, all notes with the same names as those marked are affected. This indication is called the KEY-SIGNATURE, and tells in what key the piece of music is written.

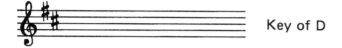

Key of D

This key-signature indicates the key of D, where all F's and C's are sharpened.

The other key-signatures usually encountered in traditional music are G, which has one sharp; A, with three sharps; and C, which has none.

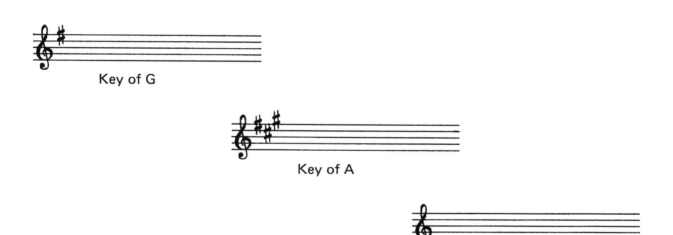

Key of G

Key of A

Key of C

Another sharp or flat, not in the key-signature but written in the music, is called an ACCIDENTAL. It affects succeeding notes of the same name, only to the end of the bar in which it occurs, or until it is cancelled by a natural sign, whichever comes first.

Denis Murphy (1910-1974)
Photograph courtesy of Mrs. Julia Mary Murphy

3. Getting Started

When you start playing, you will hold and use your hands and fingers in ways in which you probably have not done before. At first this will seem strange, and may cause you to become tense. It is essential that this does not happen. To help you remain relaxed, always remember that the fiddle and bow should never be gripped tightly. They should be held as naturally as possible, with the least effort and tension. It is important to keep in mind the fact that there is no 'one correct way' of playing traditional music, and there is no 'one correct way' of holding the instrument. The directions given should not be taken as absolutely right, but rather as guidelines.

For both hands, the fingers are numbered and designated as follows;

	THUMB	
1	FIRST	(index finger)
2	SECOND	(middle finger)
3	THIRD	(ring finger)
4	FOURTH	(little finger)

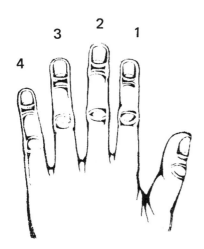 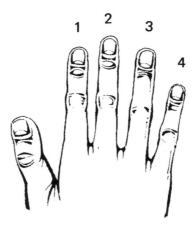

HOLDING THE FIDDLE

The fiddle is placed on the left collar-bone and is held in position between the chin, resting on the chin-rest and the left shoulder gently pressing upward on the back of the instrument. It may be necessary to use a shoulder-pad or shoulder-rest if the space between the back of the fiddle and the shoulder is too great. Ideally the shoulder should not be raised in order to hold the fiddle. Alternatively, a slightly higher chin-rest can be used.

The neck of the fiddle is held lightly between the thumb and first finger so that it is situated above the first joint of the thumb, and between the second and third joints of the first finger. The palm of the hand does not touch the neck, and is held so that it is in line with the elbow. The elbow is kept under the fiddle, and the fingers are arched over the fingerboard. When playing, the tips of the fingers are pressed firmly on the strings.

It is important that you are comfortable and confident in holding the fiddle, and that you are relaxed, particularly the wrist and fingers. When your hand gets tired, put the fiddle down and rest awhile.

HOLDING THE BOW

The thumb, which is bent slightly, is placed against the stick close to the nut. The first finger presses on the stick at the second joint, or perhaps between the first and second joints.

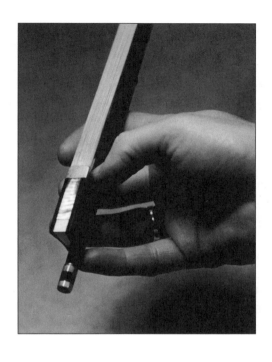

The first, second and third fingers are wrapped around the stick so that the second finger is opposite the thumb. The tip of the fourth finger touches the stick only when the lower half (nut to middle) of the bow is used and then does so to balance the bow. Since fiddle-playing mainly involves using the upper half (or two thirds) of the bow, the fourth finger spends more time off than on the stick.

Again remember the importance of being comfortable and relaxed: never grip the bow tightly.

Before starting to play, it is necessary to TUNE the fiddle. Tuning means altering the tension of the strings, each in turn, by means of the pegs or adjusters (fine tuners) to give the correct pitch. In the case of steel strings, adjusters are usually used, whereas for gut or nylon strings, the pegs are used. We have already seen that the strings are tuned in fifths – G, D, A, E.

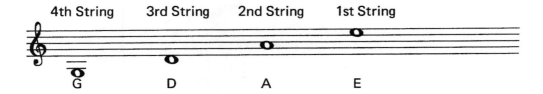

The strings are numbered 1 to 4 from the right, when the fiddle is viewed from the playing position. Fiddle-players generally refer to them by name rather than by number.

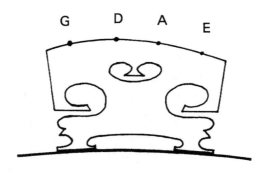

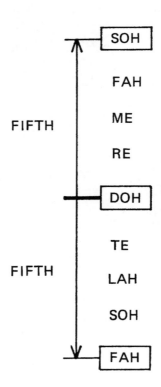

To hear what the interval of a fifth sounds like, sing the first five notes of the scale DOH, RE, ME, FAH, SOH. From DOH up to SOH is a fifth.

Now sing downward five notes DOH, TE, LAH, SOH, FAH. From DOH down to FAH is a fifth.

To begin with, you can tune the strings individually to the four notes G, D, A, E, which are played on track 1 of the demonstration CD.

The usual way however is first to tune the A string to the correct pitch, which you can obtain from a tuning fork, or another instrument such as a melodeon, tin whistle, etc.. When the A has been done, tune the D to a fifth below A, and G to a fifth below D. The E string is then tuned to a fifth above A.

At first you will probably have difficulty in recognizing the interval of a fifth, and so can use the scale to help. For example, take A as DOH and sing down to FAH which is a fifth below, to give you the pitch of the D string. Tune the other strings in like manner. Since the fifth is such a frequently occurring sound, particularly in fiddle music, you will soon be well able to recognize it, and tune your fiddle by 'ear'.

You can also tune to the four strings of another fiddle, which is in tune, or directly to the four notes G, D, A, E on a piano.

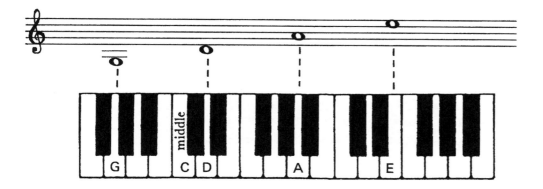

If you are still in difficulty, get your teacher or another fiddle-player to tune for you.

Now that the fiddle is in tune, and you are confident and relaxed in holding both fiddle and bow, it is time to learn how to play.

Place the middle of the bow on the A string (A is second from the right) so that it touches the string mid-way between the bridge and the end of the fingerboard. The bow should be parallel to the bridge, and always remain so when playing.

Now draw the bow firmly across the string to produce as smooth a sound as possible. With long bow strokes, move the bow alternately upward and downward. When the nut of the bow is moving away from the fiddle, the bow-stroke is called a DOWN-BOW, and when the bow moves in the opposite direction, it is called an UP-BOW. The bow direction is indicated by the signs ⊓ and ∨.

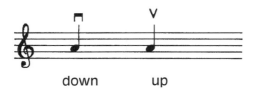

Continue to play with alternate down and up bows while ensuring that the bow remains parallel to the bridge. It is very helpful to stand in front of a mirror and watch yourself bowing, thus making it easy to see that the bow is parallel to the bridge. Good bowing technique is very important, and it is worthwhile spending time and effort in getting it right. While the wrist and fingers play a major part, it is primarily the forearm which controls bow movement. Think of the forearm as pulling the wrist, fingers and bow alternately down and up.

30

If the sound you are producing seems weak, press a little on the stick with the first finger to produce a fuller, louder sound. This use of the first finger contributes significantly to creating some of the unique characteristics of fiddle-playing – but more of that later. To bow on the open D and G strings, raise the whole right arm, and lower the arm to play E.

Play the following exercises with long bows. Count (aloud) if it helps to keep in time. Recall that the dots at the double-bar line indicate a repeat.

In the last exercise, the shorter notes (crotchets in this case) should get shorter, or perhaps faster bows.

These exercises should also be played, starting each with an up-bow.

The SCALE is a succession of eight consecutive notes – from any particular note to the note an octave higher. It is named from the note on which it begins. Starting on middle C, for example, gives the scale of C. There are both major and minor scales. In the MAJOR, the third and fourth notes, and seventh and eighth are semitones (half-tones) apart, while there are tones (whole-tones) between the remainder of the notes. The major scale corresponds to the tonic sol-fa DOH, RE, ME, FAH, SOH, LAH, TE, DOH. Thus the scale of major C is as follows;-

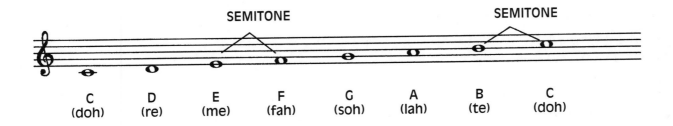

Usually the word 'major' is omitted. Thus the 'scale of C' means the
'scale of C major', and the 'key of F' is the 'key of F major'.
The first tunes we learn to play are in the key of D.

KEY OF D

The notes and fingering for the scale of D are

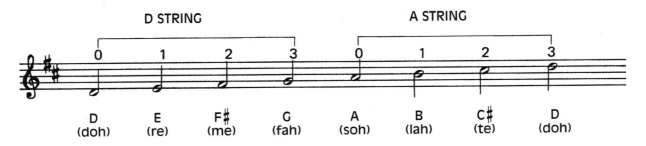

The numbers over the notes indicate the fingers to be used.
For example, 2 means the second finger, while 0 denotes the open string.
The positions on the fingerboard are

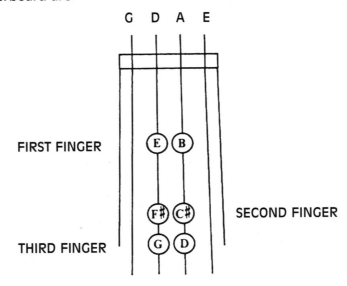

On both D and A strings, the second and third fingers are close together – this is because F♯ to G, and C♯ to D are semitones.

Since the fingering is similar for both strings, we will first concentrate on one. Play the open D string, and sing DOH to this note. Now sing RE, and adjust the position of the first finger on the string until the note you are playing (E) sounds the same as the note you are singing. Repeat this until you are sure of the correct position for the first finger. In the same way, you can learn where to place the second finger for F♯, and the third finger for G.

When you play with the second finger, the first should be kept on the string, and when playing with the third, both first and second fingers should be held in position on the string. It is also important to ensure that the fingers are pressed firmly (but not tightly) on the fingerboard. Putting all this together, play the following note sequence;–

Repeat as many times as are necessary to become very familiar with the finger positions. If you do the same on the A string, you are then in a position to play the complete scale.

The third finger on the A string gives the note D, an octave above the open D. By playing them together you can hear if they are in tune, and so check if the fingering is accurate.

Practise the following exercises, in which each note of the scale is given a separate bow.

A curved line over or under a group of notes on different lines and spaces is called a SLUR, and means that those notes should be played in one bow. Recall that a curved line over or under two notes on the same line or space is called a tie.

In the following exercises, the scale is played with different bowing patterns.

4. First Tunes

Many traditional tunes are played in the key of D, which in some respects,
can be considered the 'home' key of the fiddle. And so this is the key in which
we play the first tune, **Fáinne Geal an Lae**, a march which many will recognize.
All the notes lie within the compass of one octave, and are played on the D
and A strings only.

Fáinne Geal an Lae

(The Dawning of the Day)

It may help at first to mark the fingering, but soon you will find that this is
no longer necessary. Also, if you wish, ignore the bowings that are given,
and play one bow for each note. When you know the tune, try bowing as
indicated. You will notice that I have not marked every bow-stroke.
This is not necessary, because once you have been given the direction of
the first bow, you then play with alternate up-bows and down-bows, taking
any slurs into account.

The next piece is the air (or melody) of a song.

Níl sé ina Lá
(It is not day yet)

So far, we have played only on the D and A strings with three fingers. By using the G and E strings, as well as the fourth finger, we can get additional notes.

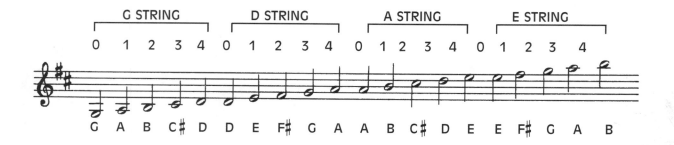

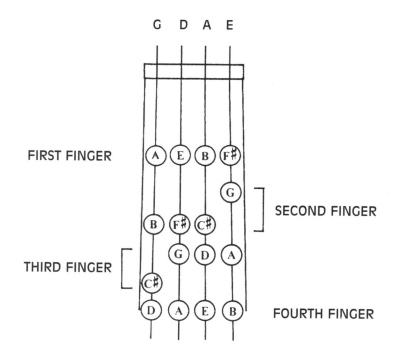

Notice that on the E string, the second finger is close to the first. To play C♯ on the G string, the third finger is stretched forward.

In the case of the fourth finger, on the G string it gives the note D, on the D string it gives A, and on the A string it gives E. However it is not used very often for these notes, because they can be played on open strings. To play B on the E string, the fourth finger should be arched over the fingerboard, and pressed firmly on the string. Even when not in use, this finger should be kept over the fingerboard.

The first dance-tune is a polka. It will probably take some time before this sounds like dance-music, having the rhythm of a polka. Later we will see that, while the notes in themselves are obviously important, it is the way in which they are played, and how the bow is used, that really makes the music. For now however, let us stay with the notes.

A Kerry Polka

Although the fourth finger is not used very often to play a note that is available on an open string, it is sometimes better to use it. In bar 3, the note A should be played with the fourth, thus avoiding the need to cross strings for one note. If you find it difficult to play in tune, use the open string, but continue to practise using the fourth.

The Munster Cloak

Another tune for your repertoire is the air of a song learned by many in school.

Báidín Fheilimí

(Feilimi's Boat)

KEY OF G

The notes and fingering in this key are

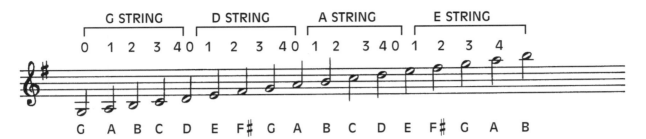

Since there is only one sharp (F♯), the positions of the fingers are slightly different from those in the key of D.

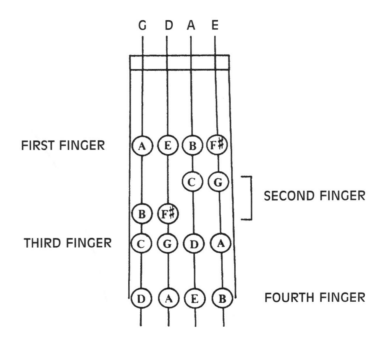

On both G and D strings, the second finger is close to the third, while on the A and E strings it is close to the first. It is very helpful to think of the individual keys in terms of the finger positions, particularly that of the second finger. This is always close to either first or third but never mid-way between. Practise the scale with various bowing patterns as you did in the key of D.

The first tune in the key of G is the air of a well-known song, **Eibhlín, a Rúin.** Notice that the last note of bar 6 and the first note of bar 7 are both played with the same finger. To give time to move the finger from one string to the other, the first note should be shortened very slightly, without losing the rhythm of the tune.

40

Eibhlín, a Rúin

(Eileen, my darling)

The next tune is a march. When you come to the repeat sign at the end of the
FIRST-TIME BAR (marked ⌐1   ⌐), go back to the previous repeat
sign at the beginning of the line to play it again. This time omit the first-time
bar, and play the SECOND-TIME BAR (⌐2   ⌐).

Amhrán Dóchais

(Song of Hope)

Dálaigh's Polka is in a minor key (or mode), but has the same key-signature as
G major. A detailed discussion on modes is outside the scope of this book.
However, from the point of view of playing, the important thing is that your
fingers 'think' in G positions, because the key-signature indicated is G.

Dálaigh's Polka

Another type of dance-tune is the jig. As I said earlier, you will probably have difficulty for the moment in making these tunes sound like dance music.
But help is available in the next chapter, and we are not too far from that now!

Túirne Mháire

(Mary's spinning-wheel)

Although Planxty Irwin has a time-signature of $\frac{6}{8}$, it is not a dance-tune, and does not have the rhythm of a jig. It is played slowly and smoothly. The last note in each of bars 7 and 15 should be shortened a little to give time to move the third finger to the D string.

Planxty Irwin

KEY OF A

Even though a large number of traditional tunes are written with a key signature of D or G, a small but significant percentage are in A.

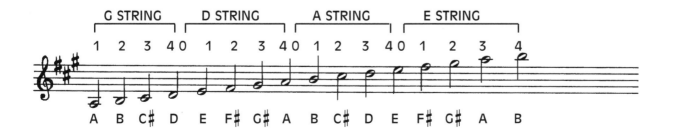

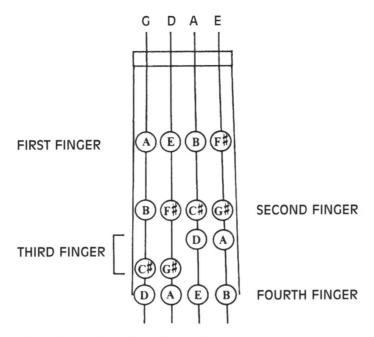

As before, practise the scale using various bowing patterns.

One Day for Recreation is a song which has the rhythm of a polka, or if you prefer, it is a polka with words.

One Day for Recreation

In bar four, the first finger is used for two consecutive notes – B and E. In some situations it is better not to move the finger from one string to the other but

44

to place it on both strings at the same time. Leave it there until the second note has been played.

This fingering should be used when a smooth transition between two notes is necessary, or when there is not enough time to move the finger from one string to the other.

KEY OF C

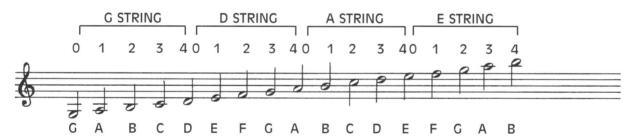

To play F on the E string, the first finger is placed near the nut.
The hand should not be moved back.

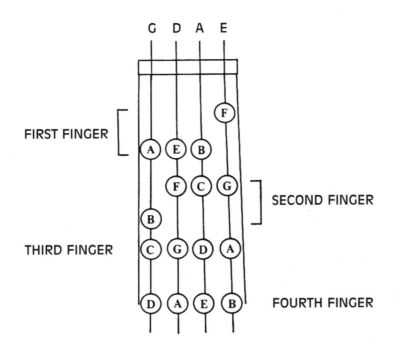

Dá bhFaighinn mo Rogha is another song with the rhythm of a polka.
In it, the singer says she would not marry the blacksmith, the tailor,
or the fisherman, choosing instead the fiddle-player when she says:
"'sé an bheileadóir is fearr liom."

Dá bhFaighinn mo Rogha
(If I had my choice)

Bowing has not been indicated: try your own.

If the singer in **Dá bhFaighinn mo Rogha** assures us of our prospects in this life, then surely **The Fiddler of Dooney** promises that a place of honour awaits us in the next!

THE FIDDLER OF DOONEY

When I play on my fiddle in Dooney,
Folk dance like a wave of the sea;
My cousin is priest in Kilvarnet,
My brother in Mocharabuiee.

I passed my brother and cousin:
They read in their books of prayer;
I read in my book of songs
I bought at the Sligo fair.

When we come at the end of time
To Peter sitting in state,
He will smile on the three old spirits,
But call me first through the gate;

For the good are always the merry,
Save by an evil chance,
And the merry love the fiddle,
And the merry love to dance:

And when the folk there spy me,
They will all come up to me,
With 'Here is the fiddler of Dooney!'
And dance like a wave of the sea.

W.B. Yeats

Paddy Killoran (1904-1965)
Photograph courtesy of Shanachie Records

48

5. Jigs

There are three types of jig, each with a different time signature –
double ($\frac{6}{8}$), slip ($\frac{9}{8}$) and single ($\frac{12}{8}$). Double jigs greatly out-number the
others, and are played more frequently, so that it is not surprising to find that,
when traditional musicians refer to 'jigs', they mean 'double jigs'. From now on,
we will do likewise.

At first, we will concentrate on bowing, and will soon realize that, while the
left-hand makes the notes, it is the bow-hand that makes the music. By this,
we mean that the characteristic rhythm, or in a word, the 'soul' of a particular
tune (jig, reel, etc.) is created by the bow-hand. This is not to say of course
that the left-hand has nothing more to contribute – far from it! Ornamentation
and variation of the melody are made possible by the left hand. But for the
moment, we will stay with the bowing.

The Connachtman's Rambles

On the CD, you will hear that this tune is not played exactly as written (or
rather, not written exactly as it is played!). The first quaver, in each group of
three, is given a very slight stress and lengthened a little, whereas the second

is shortened. In fact, if all the quavers were played exactly alike, both in duration and emphasis, the tune could scarcely be called a jig! For this reason, when reading music, you should not consider the note values given as being exact, but more an indication of the melody line which needs to be interpreted as a jig, reel, etc.. Of course, people who learn and play 'by ear' don't have any such difficulty.

Bearing all this in mind, try playing the tune, using mainly the middle third (approximately) of the bow. An accent is achieved by pressing slightly on the bow with the first finger, and at the same time, moving it a little faster.
If you find it difficult to do this, as well as playing all the notes, try just the first two bars. The symbol > over a note indicates a slight accent or stress.

 BARS 1 AND 2

It may also be helpful, in getting the emphasis right, to practise only on an open string, so that you can concentrate on the bow-hand. Play this exercise slowly at first, and gradually increase the pace. Ensure that the bow-hand and wrist remain relaxed at all times.

 OPEN STRING EXERCISE

This exercise should also be done on the other strings.

When you feel you are succeeding with the rhythm, go back and play the complete tune, which by now should start to sound like a jig.

The next tune also features the same kind of bowing. Again this time, practise the first two bars, as you did in the last jig, paying particular attention to the rhythm. In bar 4, it is better to play the note E with the fourth finger, as indicated, rather than on the open string.

50

Old John's Jig

Since traditional music is essentially melodic, it relies for much of its effect on the ORNAMENTATION, or decoration, of the melody line. The extent to which the different types of ornamentation are used varies from one fiddle-player to the next, and from one style of playing to another, but more about that later. Meanwhile, let us learn what the ornaments are, how to play them, and how to include them in the music.

The CUT, where a single grace note 'cuts' into and emphasizes the main note, is used very effectively to separate two successive notes of the same pitch: both notes being played in one bow-stroke. The grace note is obtained by a quick flick of the finger, so that it just touches the string momentarily. Try the following examples, each of which is played twice on the CD.

You may find the cut from the fourth finger to the third difficult at the moment. If so, leave it and return later.

The DOUBLE CUT is similar, except that there are two grace notes, one of which is also the main note. Again this time, the finger barely touches the string, when playing the upper grace note.

You should practise both these ornaments on all four strings.

Even though cuts involve the addition of one or more notes in a bar, the bar remains the same length, and has the same number of beats. What happens is that the grace notes 'steal' time from the notes being decorated, and so the rhythm remains unaltered. To try these ornaments in a tune, and hear how they sound, we will return to a jig already learned.

The Connachtman's Rambles

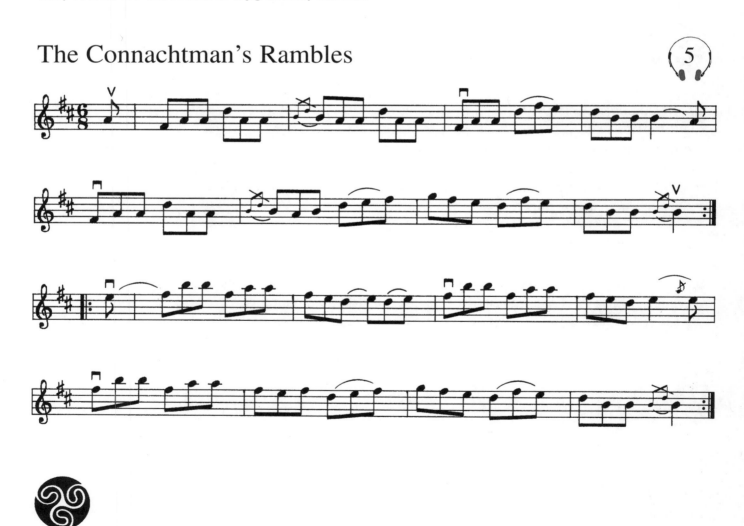

As well as including more cuts, there is another point to notice in the next tune. The first finger is used to play the last note of bar 1 and the first note of bar 2, something we met in the last chapter. In this case, the finger should be placed on both strings at the same time, and left there until the end of the second note. Make sure that both notes are in tune, by positioning the finger properly.

Gallagher's Frolics

Traditional musicians usually play each tune two or three times. It is normal (and better) to finish on a down bow. This may mean changing the bowing of the final bar, last time around. For example, to have a down bow on the last note, the end of **Gallagher's Frolics** could be played as follows;-

DOWN BOW ON LAST NOTE

You should now play the tune two or three times without stopping, and include this modification last time around.

A point to notice in the following jig is that the note C is natural, so that on the A string, the second finger has to be placed close to the first. Where F♯ follows soon after C, as in bar 2, take care to ensure that the second finger is forward for F♯, and back for C.

The Hag's Purse

And so to the ROLL, which is the most widely used type of ornament. Two auxiliary notes, one above and one below, decorate the main note, usually a dotted crotchet, in a five-note sequence, in which all the notes are played in the same bow stroke. To hear what rolls sound like in the context of a tune, listen to **The Rambling Pitchfork** (track 8 and page 56), the next jig we will learn. First let us find out how to play a roll on F♯, second finger on D.

ROLL ON F♯

The upper auxiliary note (G) is played with a flick of the third finger, as in the cut. To play the lower note (E), it is necessary to lift the second finger momentarily. Remember that, while the note values indicated are approximately correct, they should not be considered exact. In this case, that is even more true, as the relative lengths of notes in a roll can vary from one fiddle-player to another. Only by listening is it possible to get any idea of what a roll should sound like. The effect is rhythmic, and so it is helpful to think of it as such, rather than as a melodic sequence of five notes.

Since a roll on the third finger involves the fourth or weak finger, we will leave it for the present, and concentrate on the other fingers. Notice that a roll, in this form at least, is not possible on an open string. In the case of a roll on the first finger, the upper note may be played either by the second or third finger, whichever you find easier. Practise these examples slowly at first, and then gradually increase the speed.

When you feel more confident, play the following note-patterns, where the symbol ∞ over a note indicates a roll.

You should also play these examples on the other strings, before trying the next jig.

The Rambling Pitchfork

If you are having difficulty playing the rolls in time, try them individually.
For example, play the first two bars slowly a number of times. It is a good idea,
when learning something new, to practise the difficult parts, one or two bars at
a time.

Another point to bear in mind is that, even when not in use, the fingers should
always be close to the fingerboard, and in some situations, one finger is kept on
a particular note. In bars 1 and 2 (also 4 and 5), try to ensure that the second
finger remains on the D string, from the end of the roll to the last F♯ in the next
bar. This is sometimes indicated by a line placed over these notes.

BARS 1 AND 2

At first you may not find this easy to do, particularly when playing the open A,
because of the second finger touching this string. However with practice, you
will learn to position the finger so that this does not happen. An easier example
is found in bars 11 and 12.

BARS 11 AND 12

The use of this type of fingering helps to improve playing technique, and keep the music in tune. As we will see later, there are other advantages. It is a good habit to develop, and should be used when possible.

The Lark on the Strand gives further opportunity to use the same kind of fingering (in bars 3 and 11 for example), and also includes cuts and rolls. Notice that the C♯ in bar 12 is an accidental, and so the note C is sharpened only in that bar.

The Lark on the Strand

Remember to play the last note on a down bow, when finishing the tune.

In bars 10 and 14 of **The Rose in the Heather**, a cut with the fourth finger is used to decorate the note A. Practise this before playing the tune, to ensure that the effect is the same as a cut with any of the other fingers. If you have difficulty, and wish to leave it for the present, play the tune without this ornament.

Another point to notice is that in order to play the C♯ in bar 8, the third finger on the G string is stretched forward. If in doubt about this, check the fingerboard chart on page 36.

The Rose in the Heather

In the next jig, bar 6 includes C♮ and C♯: ensure that the second finger is placed correctly for both notes. On the repeat of each part, the first-time bar is omitted and the second-time bar is played instead.

The High Part of the Road

By now you will notice that we have played rolls only on dotted crotchets. Later, we will also use them on crotchets. It is not necessary to play a roll every time, although I have indicated that in the tunes learned so far. Instead, a dotted crotchet can be replaced by three quavers, with the middle one higher or lower. For example, the first bar of **The High Part of the Road** can be played as follows;-

ALTERNATIVE FOR BAR 1

Slip jigs differ from double jigs in that there are three beats in the bar. While the rhythm and bowing are similar, the musical feeling is distinctive. The next tune gives an opportunity to hear this.

Give us a Drink of Water

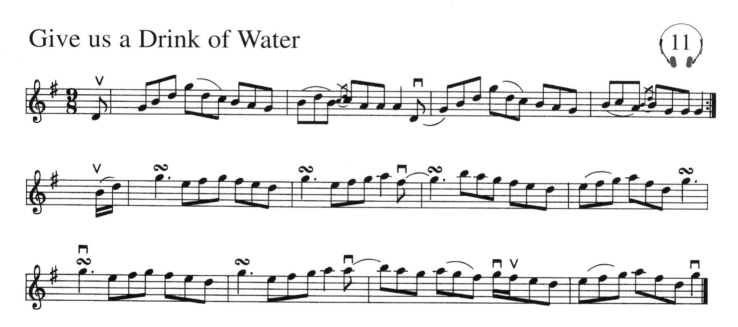

Remember that all traditional musicians learn and play 'by ear': the sooner you can do that, the better! This is not as difficult as it seems because, within each tune, there are recurring bars and phrases. Generally, each part consists of two four-bar sections that are often similar, sometimes identical. For example in the last tune, there is very little difference between the two phrases which comprise the second part. Because of this, tunes can easily be memorized, particularly if they are practised in sections of two or four bars at a time. With experience, this will no longer be necessary, and tunes can be learned very quickly.

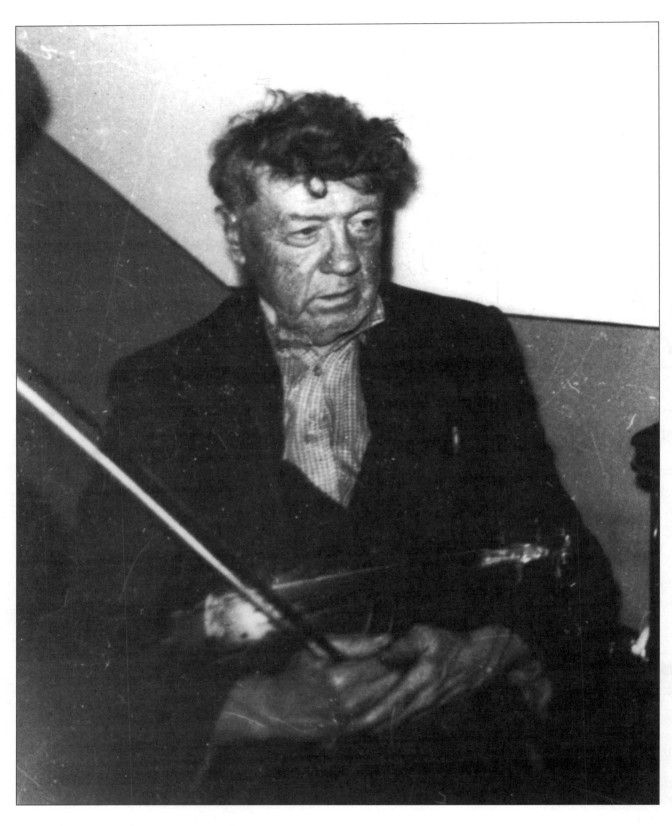

Pádraig O'Keeffe (1888-1963)
Photograph courtesy of Dan O'Connell

6. Slides and Polkas

Even though strictly speaking, slides are single jigs, we will consider them in this chapter along with polkas, rather than in the previous chapter on jigs. We do this, because both types of tune are very much associated with the dancing of sets (or set-dancing), and so in a sense, always go together.

A SET (formerly known as a 'Set of Quadrilles') consists of a number of fixed dance-figures, arranged in a sequence of parts (usually five). A short break is normally made between parts. It is danced by four couples, positioned in the form of a square. There are many different sets, each with its particular pattern of dance-figures. They are generally known by the place-name of origin, for example, **The Ballycommon Set**, and **The Cuil Aodha Set**. A set which uses the same rhythm for all its parts may also be known as a 'reel set', 'jig set', or 'polka set', as may be the case. Approximately half the total number of sets have mixed rhythms. **The North Kerry Set**, for example, has polkas for parts one and two, the third is a slide, the fourth another polka, and the fifth is a 'hop' (or fast) hornpipe. This type of hornpipe is also known as a 'hoppy'. The word 'slide' derives from a sliding movement of the dancers. Through usage, it has come to mean the music that is played, as well as the dance itself. The term 'single jig' is rarely used now in this context.

Village-dancing in Ventry, Co. Kerry c. 1890
Photograph courtesy 'Collection Ireland'

SLIDES

In the slide, the duration of the beat is a dotted crotchet, as in the jig.
However the note pattern for each beat is mainly crotchet and quaver (♩ ♪),
and to a lesser extent, three quavers (♫♪), whereas in the jig, as we have
already seen, the reverse is very much the case. This gives the slide a very
different and distinctive feeling: it has a great 'swing', which can be heard in
Mick Duggan's Slide. The time-signature is $\frac{12}{8}$, with four beats in the bar.

Mick Duggan's Slide

Before playing this tune, there are some points to be made about the bowing.
Short bow-strokes should be used for detached quavers (in other words,
quavers which are not slurred), for example, those at the beginning of bar 2.
This has the effect of giving the correct emphasis to the rhythm. Note also
that the last quaver of one beat is, at times, slurred with the next beat,
giving bowing patterns of

To illustrate these points, and help with the rhythm, practise the following
exercises;-

When you feel confident, try **Mick Duggan's Slide**. Notice that the first bar of the second part includes the note G♯ on the E string. Remember that in this case, the second finger needs to be forward.

The next tune gives further opportunity for the same kind of bowing. In bar 5, a cut is used to decorate the note A: it is achieved in exactly the same manner as in the last chapter. Practise this separately, if necessary.

Denis Murphy's Slide (1)

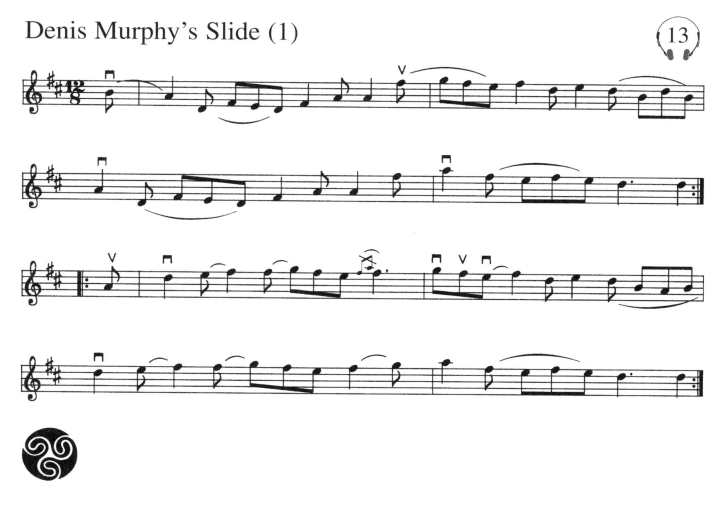

In bar 2 of **The Brosna Slide**, a crotchet down-bow is followed by an up-bow with four quavers. To ensure that you don't run-out of bow before the end of the bar, the crotchet should get approximately the same length of bow as the other four notes together. Move the bow faster on the down-bow.

The Brosna Slide

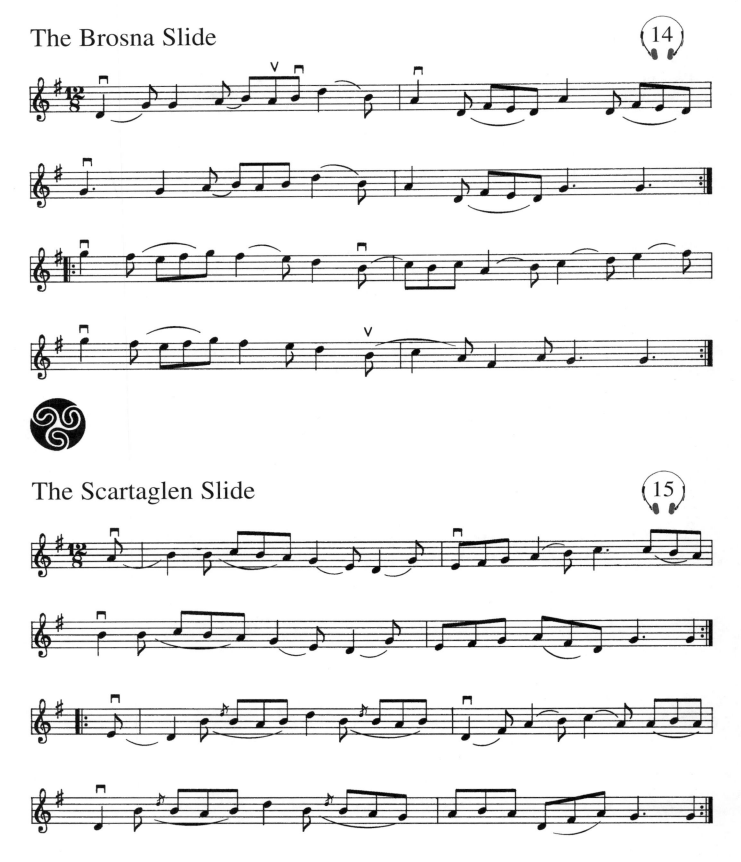

The Scartaglen Slide

Traditional music is normally played in sets of two or three tunes in which, as we have already seen, each is repeated once or twice. When you know **The Scartaglen Slide**, play the previous two in succession, without a stop: they go well together. Don't forget to finish the set on a down-bow. This will mean modifying the end of the second tune last time around, for example as follows;-

DOWN-BOW ON LAST NOTE

By now you will have noticed that in the tunes played so far, both first and second parts are repeated. The next slide is different in this respect, because the second part is twice as long as the first, and so is not repeated.

The Clog

POLKAS

The characteristic rhythm of the polka is very much different from what we have already had: to hear this, listen to **The Top of Maol** (track 16 and page 67). The second and fourth quavers in each bar are emphasised slightly. Since the beat is placed on quavers one and three, the stress (or accent) is then said to be on the 'off-beat'.

At first this may cause some difficulty with the bowing, because in many cases, the accent comes in the second half of the bow-stroke. To help with this, practise the following exercises – the second one is unmarked. Recall that an accent is achieved by pressing slightly on the bow with the first finger, and at the same time, moving it a little faster.

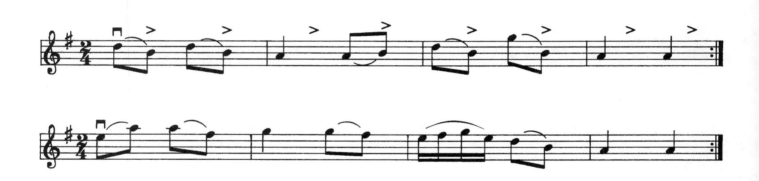

At the beginning of the previous chapter, when starting to play jigs, I told you to use mainly the middle third of the bow. I assume that, at this stage, you are using more of the bow when necessary. If not, it is time to do so !

And so to **The Top of Maol**. Notice that, in bars 3 and 11, the last semiquaver is slurred in one bow with the succeeding two notes. The last quaver of bar 14 is also bowed in a similar manner. Don't forget to shorten the last note of bar 2 very slightly to give time to move the third finger to the D string.

The Top of Maol

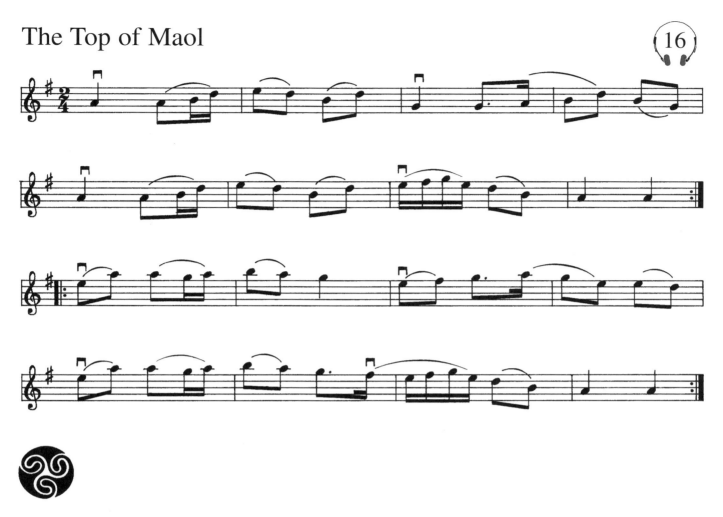

The next polka features the same kind of bowing. In bar 10, the last of the four semiquavers, being on a different string, is slurred with the two notes which follow.

Séan McGoverns Polka

A point of interest in the next tune, **Art O'Keeffe's Polka**, is the key-signature.
Since the tune begins and ends on the note A, and has a 'feeling' of the key of
A about it when played, it appears to be in that key. Traditional musicians
certainly consider it to be in the key of A. One would therefore expect G♯ in
the key-signature: however, because the note G does not occur in the tune,
it cannot be sharpened! Therefore the key-signature is as indicated.
Furthermore, the note D does not occur, so that only five notes of the scale
are used – A, B, C♯, E, F♯. This is referred to as a PENTATONIC scale.

Art O'Keeffe's Polka

Earlier in the book, you learned **Dálaigh's Polka** (page 42). At the time I said
that you probably would have difficulty making it sound like dance music.
Well, we now play the tune again and try to rectify that! As well as including
some ornamentation, the bowing is changed. The accent, of course, continues
to be on the 'off beat'. Notice that in bar 12, a crotchet note is replaced by a
quaver note followed by a rest. This is very effective on an up-bow,
particularly if the bow is raised a little off the string at the end of the note.

Dálaigh's Polka

So far, the bowing for polkas has consisted mostly of two bows per bar, with a slight emphasis in the second half of the bow-stroke. By now you should be familiar with this, and not have any great difficulty. It is time to introduce some variations. In **The Lakes of Sligo**, notes in the second half of bars 3, 5 and 10 get separate bows: these should be played with short bow-strokes. Let me remind you again to keep your fingers on the fingerboard as much as possible, and raise them only when necessary. By keeping the first finger on the E string, from F♯ at the end of bar 11 to the beginning of bar 13, you will ensure that the hand does not move, when you stretch the fourth finger to play B.

The Lakes of Sligo

Next we will play **The Top of Maol** again, this time with some ornamentation and changes in bowing.

The Top of Maol

This gives an idea of how variation in bowing can impart additional 'lift' and excitement, while still maintaining the essential feeling of the tune.

The next and final polka in this chapter goes well with the last one as a set of tunes. When you know it, try to play both together, as on track 20 of the CD. Don't forget to modify the bowing last time around to finish on a down-bow.

The Scartaglen Polka

Michael Coleman (1891-1945)
Photograph courtesy of Shanachie Records

7. Hornpipes

The time signature indicated is $\frac{4}{4}$ or **C**. However it is usual, in the case of hornpipes and reels, to count two beats per bar, on the first and third crotchets.

We have seen earlier that the note-values, as written, should not be considered exact, but rather an indication of the melody line. In that respect, the hornpipe is no different. Even though a dotted rhythm (♩. ♪) is shown, the note-values, as played, lie somewhere between this and even quavers: the rhythm is dotted, but not to the extent indicated by the notation. This will become clear on listening to **The Boys of Bluehill**.

The Boys of Bluehill

In bar 2, there are three quavers with the number 3 placed over them. This is called a TRIPLET. Even though three quavers are written, they occupy the same length of time as two quavers. Triplets are frequently used in place of two notes a third apart. In this case, B and D are replaced by the triplet B, C♯, D.

BASIC MELODY, BAR 2

TRIPLET ORNAMENT, BAR 2

There are other examples of this ornament in the tune, and each can be slurred in one bow or, to give more emphasis, bowed with short bow-strokes. Try both to compare how they sound.

The second part of this hornpipe gives a fine opportunity for keeping the first finger on the fingerboard, from F♯ at the beginning through to the middle of bar 11.

BARS 9 TO 11

It is now time to return to the previous page to play the first version of **The Boys of Bluehill**. Remember that, in bars 7 and 15, a down-bow should be given approximately the same length of bow as the three succeeding notes together on an up-bow.

By now you will probably begin to realize that while the bow-hand gives the rhythm to the tune, there is no 'one way' of bowing. We saw this in the last chapter when I gave an alternative bowing for **The Top of Maol**. As a further example of this, we will play **The Boys of Bluehill** again, but with some changes in bowing. Don't forget to modify the bowing of the final bar last time around, to finish on a down-bow. When you have played the tune both ways, you may have a preference for one version, or perhaps you may wish to combine ideas from both. This is fine so long as the tune remains a hornpipe!

The Boys of Bluehill

In the next tune, **The Little Stack of Barley**, triplets are used in a different way. In bar 9, for example, a crotchet is replaced by a triplet, with the middle quaver one note higher than the other two.

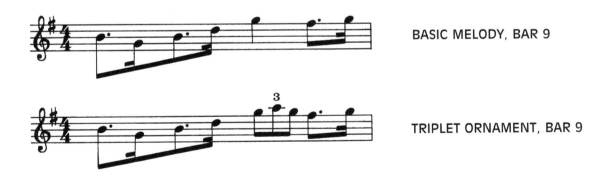

BASIC MELODY, BAR 9

TRIPLET ORNAMENT, BAR 9

Like the earlier examples, these triplets can be slurred, or bowed separately for added emphasis. In the case of bowed triplets, I have indicated ⊓ ∨ ⊓ (Down-Up-Down), because I usually play this way myself. Some fiddle-players bow triplets ∨ ⊓ ∨. To try this, you will need to change the bowing for the preceding notes, so that you start the triplet on an up-bow. When you know this tune, you may wish to try some bowing variations, as we did in the previous tune.

The Little Stack of Barley

The next hornpipe goes well with the previous one, when both are played together as a set: play Cronin's Hornpipe as the first of the two.

Cronin's Hornpipe

A point to notice in **Cronin's Hornpipe** is that the melody line of bars 1 and 2 occurs again in bars 5 and 6, and also in bars 13 and 14. To introduce some contrast, bar 6 could be played differently. Two possible variations are as follows;-

ALTERNATIVE VARIATIONS IN BAR 6

Alternatively, a long G with a roll could be played. Try these variations, and decide for yourself whether or not to include them.

An interesting feature in the following hornpipe is that the note C appears in both sharpened and natural forms, in bar 4 for example. This is called INFLECTION (where the note C is said to be inflected), and occurs in a small but significant percentage of tunes. Make sure, when playing this bar, that the second finger is placed correctly in each case, back for C♮ and forward for C♯.

Chief O'Neill's Favourite

The triplet in bar 8 can also be played with the note A instead of G.
Play A with the fourth finger.

ALTERNATIVE FOR BAR 8

This may need some practice so that the A sounds clear.

The next tune includes examples of TREBLING, a form of ornamentation which
uses the bow. Three notes of the same pitch are played in a triplet pattern.
They are bowed separately with short bow-strokes, which are achieved mainly
by wrist action. The bowing indicated is ⊓ ∨ ⊓, because this is how I bow
trebles: if you prefer, try ∨ ⊓ ∨ .

Trebles are frequently used on open strings, because rolls, in the strict
sense, are not possible. The use of the word 'treble' in this context differs
significantly from its use in 'treble clef'.

The Kildare Fancy

23

Since the notes in the second last bar (bar 15) alternate between the E and A strings, a rocking movement of the bow is necessary. This can be achieved by various alternative bowing patterns. Later when we come to playing reels, we will also find similar note sequences, and consequently, similar bowing. It is therefore worthwhile at this stage considering some of these bowing patterns.

The first has separate bow-strokes for each note, and begins on a down-bow. It is helpful to watch the movement of the wrist and forearm in a mirror. An anti-clockwise circular pattern is clearly evident. If the circle is kept small, the rhythm is better.

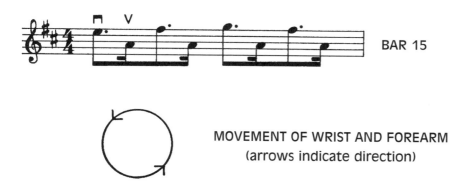

BAR 15

MOVEMENT OF WRIST AND FOREARM
(arrows indicate direction)

When the first note is on an up-bow, the wrist moves in a clockwise circular direction.

Next, the notes are bowed in pairs, not in a 1 & 2, 3 & 4 sequence, but rather in a 1, 2 & 3, 4 & 1 pattern. This produces a figure-of-eight movement, which should be smooth, and like the circle, kept small.

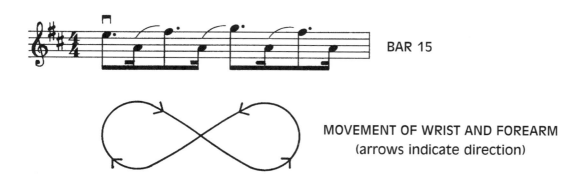

BAR 15

MOVEMENT OF WRIST AND FOREARM
(arrows indicate direction)

By starting with an up-bow, the pattern is still figure-of-eight, but in the opposite direction.

To hear how they sound in context, play The **Kildare Fancy** using these bowing variations in turn. The bowing indicated for bar 15 in the tune itself is a combination of separate and slurred notes.

SET DANCES are so-called because they have a set (or fixed) sequence of dance-steps. The rhythm is generally that of a hornpipe, with a time-signature of $\frac{4}{4}$. A smaller number of set-dances are in $\frac{6}{8}$, thus having the rhythm of a jig. The number of bars in each part, particularly the second, is frequently not eight, as in the other dance-tunes, but twelve. **Rodney's Glory** is one such set-dance. This use of the word 'set' should not be confused with that in 'set-dancing'.

Rodney's Glory

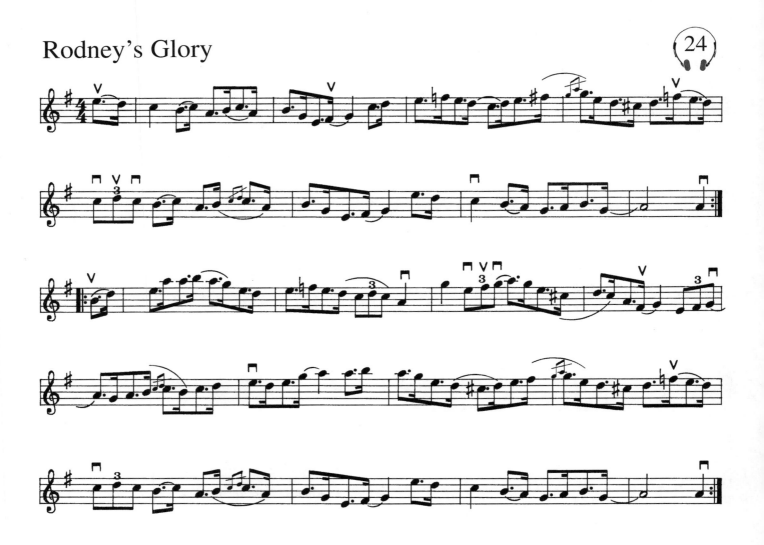

8. Reels

Among traditional musicians, the reel is undoubtedly the most popular type of tune. At concerts and particularly sessions, reels far out-number the other dance tunes. In addition, almost all records and collections of instrumental music feature more reels than anything else. Like the other dance tunes, it has its own characteristic rhythm. While the time-signature is $\frac{4}{4}$ or $\mathbf{C}$, as in the hornpipe, a slight accent or 'lift' is given to the second and fourth crotchets in each bar.

Anything for John Joe? is our first reel. I have not included ornamentation, so that you can concentrate on the rhythm, which in effect means the bowing. Before playing the tune, let us consider the fingering and bowing of the first bar.

FINGERING IN BAR 1

The second finger should be kept on the D string (F♯) while the open A is being played. Similarly, the third finger should be kept on the string while B is being played. We met this idea earlier, and by now you should be able to position both second and third fingers, so that they do not touch the A string while it is being played.

BOWING IN BAR 1

Since the first down-bow has to cross strings (D to A) for one note, the bow-arm should be lowered only as far as is necessary to reach the A string. At the same time, press slightly on the bow with the first finger to stress this note (A) a little. The second half of the bar is similar, because it is necessary to cross strings for the note B.

By bowing like this, and at the same time keeping the fingers on the strings,

you will achieve smooth and relaxed string-crossing, as well as ensuring
the correct rhythmic emphasis. Practise this bar well before trying the rest
of the tune.

Anything for John Joe ?

When you start to play, you will notice that bars 3, 5 and 7 are the same as
bar 1. The bowing pattern in some of the other bars is also quite similar,
so that when you succeed in getting the first bar right, the remainder is not
too difficult !

In the first bar of the next reel, you will see that a down-bow with only one
note is followed by an up-bow with three quavers. There is a similar situation
in bar 2, and in other bars throughout the tune.

BOWING IN BARS 1 AND 2

We have already met this type of bowing. However in this case, the down-
bows have the effect of placing a slight emphasis on the off-beats (beats 2
and 4), thus imparting a 'lift' to the melody. Practise these bars, and you will
see that in the first, the wrist and forearm move in an anti-clockwise circular
pattern – try to keep the circle small.

The Peeler's Jacket

If you find the rolls too difficult to play at first, omit them for the moment by playing bar 9 as follows;-

ALTERNATIVE FOR BAR 9

However, they should be included as soon as possible.

The triplet at the end of bar 11 will probably need some attention to ensure that the bow and fingers change at the same time, so that the notes sound clear. It will help if the first note is emphasized very slightly. Remember that short bow-strokes are produced mainly by wrist movement. Notice also that the last note of the triplet is slurred across the bar-line with the next note.

When you have learned **The Peeler's Jacket**, try the following version of the first part, in which I have made some changes to the bowing. In particular, notice the up-bow at the beginning of the first bar. This involves crossing strings for one note, something we already met: it is played in exactly the same way this time. When you know this version, you may wish to use it in place of the first part as already given, or indeed, you may like to combine ideas from both.

The Peeler's Jacket   (first part with alternative bowing)

The next reel has more examples of having to cross strings to play one note.
In the first bar, the bow-arm is raised to play E, while in bar 3, it is lowered to
play B. As already pointed out, the arm should be lowered, or raised as the
case may be, only as far as is necessary. Another point to notice is that the last
note of bar 12 (G) has to be cut very slightly short, so that there is
sufficient time to move the third finger to the E string for the next note (A).

The Old Copperplate

To introduce some variation in bar 13, which is the same as bar 9, the
crotchet A is decorated with a treble. We saw in the last chapter on hornpipes,
that a treble is bowed with short bow strokes achieved mostly by wrist action.
This is even more the case when playing reels, because they are faster.

In fact, little more than a flick of the wrist is all that is necessary to produce the correct bow movement. You will know that the trebling is right when you can hear, not so much the individual notes of the treble, but rather a rhythmic 'lift' being given to the tune.

When starting a tune (or set of tunes), traditional musicians very often play a note or two as a lead-in or introduction. Generally this is not shown on the written music. It is normal when finishing, to lengthen the last note, and this may be indicated by a PAUSE sign (⌒). Both these points can be heard in **Jackie Coleman's Reel**. Notice also that on the last note, I play two notes! This is called DOUBLE-STOPPING (or double-stringing), in other words, playing on two strings simultaneously. Since the last note of the reel is D (third finger on A string), it is easy to play the open D string, an octave lower, at the same time. This is shown by having two notes on the same stem.

DOUBLE-STOPPED PAUSE
ON LAST NOTE

Double-stopping is a very effective ornament which can be used in different ways, and so is something about which we will have more to say later.

Jackie Coleman's Reel

85

We have seen earlier that the type of bowing indicated in bar 2 for example, causes the bow-arm to move in a figure-of-eight pattern. If, while bowing like this, you keep the second finger on the D string for the duration of the bar, the effect achieved is that of a melody line consisting of the first quaver of each pair, with the F♯ notes serving as a kind of drone underneath. Since bar 3 is similar, it is worth spending some time practicing these two bars together. In bar 3, the first finger remains on both the D and A strings for the duration of the bar.

In addition to decorating individual notes, as we have done so far, a traditional musician will at times vary the melody itself. This is called MELODIC VARIATION. Bar 11 of **Jackie Coleman's Reel** can be played as follows;-

ALTERNATIVE FOR BAR 11

When you know the tune, you can include this alternative, occasionally. If bar 11 were played like this all the time, there would no longer be any variation! Remember that ornamentation and melodic variation are an integral part of the music.

Drowsy Maggie

Drowsy Maggie features extensive string-crossing in the first part, enabling you to apply what you have learned in the last reel. The parts are not repeated, and so it is played SINGLE. When the parts of a tune are repeated, as is generally the case, it is said to be played DOUBLE. Ending this reel as written is very abrupt. To finish last time around, it is usual to add an extra note.

END OF TUNE

When the second of a pair of quavers is followed by a crotchet of the same pitch, they can be tied together to make them effectively a dotted crotchet. A roll can then be played to ornament this note.

ROLL ON TIED NOTES

These are featured in the second part.

The Humours of Tulla

Although separate bows are indicated for all the triplets, this does not have to be the case. Bar 12, for instance, could be played as follows;-

ALTERNATIVE BOWING
IN BARS 11 AND 12

You may like to do the same for some of the other triplets, and compare the musical effect by playing them both ways.

A roll, as we have played it so far, cannot be used on an open string. But a modified form, with the two auxiliary notes above the main note, is possible.

ROLL ON OPEN STRING

Like the other rolls, the upper note, G in this case, is played with a quick flick of the third finger. The effect is rhythmic rather than melodic, and the same symbol (∽) is used. The following version of **The Woman of the House** includes these rolls in both first and second parts.

The Woman of the House

The triplet in the first bar can be omitted while learning the tune, by playing a crotchet C instead. However, try to include it as soon as possible. Bar 5 is similar.

ALTERNATIVE FOR BAR 1

On the CD, you will hear that the first crotchet in bar 8 (and also bar 16) is at times cut short, almost clipped. We met this idea already in **Dálaigh's Polka**. In a reel, it is equally effective as an up-bow ornament, with the bow being either raised slightly off the string, or stopped on it.

In bars 3 and 10 of **Dublin Porter**, cuts using the fourth finger are indicated. Since this is the 'weak' finger, and also because reels are faster, you will need to practise these bars, to ensure that the effect is similar to that obtained with the other fingers.

Dublin Porter

When finishing this tune last time around, play the final bar as follows, to end on a down bow.

END OF TUNE

The Humours of Carrigaholt includes a roll on the third finger in bar 11, and also in bar 13. This involves using the fourth finger for the upper auxiliary note, and so may need extra practice, to get the same rhythmic effect as with rolls on the other fingers. The lower auxiliary note should be a semitone below, C♯ in this case.

ROLL ON D

The triplets in bars 2 and 6 are slurred, thus contrasting with those in the last tune, where the notes got separate bows. In bar 12, we meet another example of double-stopping, in which the open E and A strings are played together. The musical interval is a fifth, which allows you to hear if the fiddle is out of tune! It is better not to include it each time, but rather occasionally to ornament the melody note E in this manner.

The Humours of Carrigaholt

Rolls and trebles are often interchangeable. For example, bar 11 (and bar 13) could be played with a treble on the crotchet D, as follows;–

ALTERNATIVE ORNAMENTATION IN BAR 11

When you know the tune, try both types of ornamentation to hear how they sound. The extent to which a fiddle-player uses rolls rather than trebles, or vice versa, is a personal matter. This depends largely on the style of playing, about which more will be said later.

A GLISSANDO, or SLIDE, involves sliding the finger along the finger-board, usually from the note a semitone lower, up to the note to be played. It is sometimes indicated by an arrow (———>) over the note. This 'slide' should not be confused with the dance of the same name. In bar 4 of the next reel, a slide from F up to F♯ is very effective.

SLIDE IN BAR 1

The length and duration of a slide are matters of personal taste, but generally they are short rather than long.

The Moving Bog

91

When the last note of **The Moving Bog** is played, there is a feeling that the music is not finished, almost as if the tune 'wants' to be played again. And if it is, the same thing happens once more! The solution in a case like this is to follow with another one. The next reel goes well in that respect, and both can be played together as a set.

In bar 8 of **The Man of the House**, a roll is indicated on the last note. You may have some difficulty with this, because the note has to be made minutely shorter to give time for the bow to cross to the E string for the next note. Alternatively, a cut between the quaver and crotchet can be played, similar to what is done in the final bar. Try playing both ways. The bowing pattern of bars 13 and 14 has three notes on an up-bow, and one on a down-bow. The rhythmic articulation which this kind of bowing produces is once again evident.

The Man of the House

(32)

To finish this tune last time around, play an extra note or, better still, two double-stopped notes.

DOUBLE-STOPPING
ON LAST NOTE

The musical interval produced by these two notes is a fourth. Ensure that the second finger on the G string (B) is clear of the D string.

Earlier I mentioned that melodic variation is an inherent part of the music.
To give some further examples, we will try a number of variations in the
melody of this reel.

The Piper's Despair

The first variation is in bar 12, which can be played thus;-

ALTERNATIVE FOR BAR 12

Play the second part of the tune a number of times, and include this
occasionally to hear the difference.

We can also introduce a change in the melody of bars 3 and 4, giving an
open-string roll on the first D.

ALTERNATIVE FOR
BARS 3 AND 4

Since a treble and roll are interchangeable, these bars can also
be played as follows;-

ALTERNATIVE FOR BARS 3 AND 4

Try all these variations in turn to hear how they sound, and decide for yourself
whether or not to include them.

In the first bar of **The Old Pigeon on the Gate**, the third finger should be kept
on the note G to the end of the bar.

FINGERING FOR BAR 1

In order to play the note D, you can either tilt the hand until the third finger
makes contact with the A string, or flatten this finger to achieve the same
result. Better still, combine both: tilt the hand slightly, and at the same time,
flatten the third finger a little. It helps greatly if, when the third finger is
placed on the D string at the beginning of the bar, it is as close as possible to,
but not touching the A string.

The Old Pigeon on the Gate

In bar 14, a double-stopped dotted crotchet can be played in place of three
quavers.

DOUBLE - STOPPING IN BAR 14

The musical interval produced this time is a major third. If the second finger is
kept on the string, as indicated, there should not be much difficulty playing in
tune. Another possibility is to play an open-string roll on this dotted crotchet.

ROLL IN BAR 14

The next two reels incorporate much of what we have learned so far.
They go well together as a set, each tune being played three or four times
(even though on the CD, this is not the case). Try to vary the ornamentation
and melody, at least occasionally.

The Pretty Girls of Mayo

The end of the first reel should be modified when leading into the second tune. To finish the set, play a double-stopped pause on the final D.

Rolling on the Ryegrass

At this stage of the book, I suggest that while working through the next
chapter, you also go back over all the tunes learned so far, starting with jigs.
Since you are now more of a fiddle-player than when you started, you should
be better able to play them, with more confidence, more ornamentation,
better rhythm, and of course, from memory.

9. Airs

Airs can conveniently be divided into two categories. SLOW AIRS are the melodies of the songs sung by sean-nós singers. Since the melody line follows the phrasing of the text rather than the framework of a fixed time-signature, these airs generally have a free musical metre. On the other hand, tunes such as those composed by CAROLAN are mainly instrumental, and do have definite time-signatures.

Carolan, the last of the Irish harper-composers, was born in 1670 in County Meath. As a child he migrated with his parents to County Roscommon, where his father was employed by the MacDermott Roe family. At the age of eighteen, having become totally blind through illness, Carolan was placed by his patroness, Mrs. MacDermott Roe, under the tutelage of a harper. Three years later, she provided him with a horse and money, and he set out on his life as an itinerant harper. For nearly fifty years, he travelled throughout Ireland, entertaining his patrons while staying in their houses, and composing pieces of music in their honour. Two such tunes are **Planxty Irwin**, which you learned in Chapter 4, and **Henry MacDermott Roe**, No 101 in Appendix A. Coming towards the end of his life, he returned to the house of the MacDermott Roe family, where he died in 1738.

The time signature for **Sheebeg and Sheemore** is $\frac{6}{4}$, which is similar to $\frac{6}{8}$, except that there are six crotchets, or their equivalent, in each bar. They are in groups of three, with the beat on the first and fourth crotchets.

To hear less of the piano, turn the stereo balance control to the right.

Sheebeg and Sheemore

Try to get the bowing as smooth as possible, with long bow-strokes.
In bars 6 and 13, when crossing from the D string to the E string, the bow should be raised slightly, so that it does not touch the A string. I have included some ornamentation: you may like to try some more, as long as it does not change the character of the music.

When you know the tune, it is time to consider the question of VIBRATO, where the finger rocks back and forth on the string, at a rate which creates a throbbing effect without noticeable change in pitch. Listen to **Sheebeg and Sheemore** to hear this, particularly on the long notes. Vibrato is used to give added expression to a melody, and in a sense, may be considered an ornament, which can emphasize certain notes or phrases. How is it produced?

With the hand loose and relaxed, gently move the wrist and forearm (mainly the wrist) back and forth to achieve a slight rocking motion of the finger on the string, thus causing the pitch of the note to oscillate. The farther the finger rocks back and forth, the wider the vibrato is said to be, and the more intense it sounds. Speed and width are both matters of personal musical taste. Generally speaking, a very wide and continuous vibrato is out of character with traditional music.

Try it first on individual notes, using the second or third fingers, and you will find that it is not at all easy to do! It will take quite a long time to master, and so it is helpful to watch, and listen to other fiddle-players: guidance from your teacher is also of great assistance.

In the next tune, don't feel completely tied to the bowing as indicated. Try to vary the ornamentation, and add other decorations. Remember to watch the wrist-patterns of the bow-hand in bars 13 and 14, to achieve smooth string crossing.

Carolan's Draught

On the long E in bar 16, you can play a unison double-stop. This means playing the note on the open E string, as well as with the fourth finger on the A string. Alternatively, the third finger can be used to slide from D, the previous note, up to E. In either case, the finger must not touch the E string. Unison double-stopping is indicated by two stems on the double-stopped note.

UNISON DOUBLE - STOP
IN BAR 16

Play this note both ways to hear the difference.

In bar 15 of **Planxty Drury**, the first two notes are played in the same bow, but with a very slight break between them. This is achieved by stopping the bow momentarily on the string, and is indicated by a short line under each note.

Planxty Drury

The musical phrasing of a slow air follows the metre of the text, and so in writing the tune, it may not fit comfortably into a fixed time-signature. There is no doubt that the best way to learn an air is by listening to it being sung or played, and using the written notation as an aid, only when necessary.

The first phrase of **Cáit Ní Dhuibhir** ends in bar 4 on the note E, after which there is a slight break before going on to the next phrase. The same happens at the end of each subsequent phrase. This is similar to the punctuation breaks which occur in spoken language, where the meaning is frequently conveyed by the way it is said, as much as by what is said.

Cáit Ní Dhuibhir
(Kitty O Dwyer)

In order to concentrate on the melody and phrasing, I have indicated little ornamentation. This can be included later.

When Tomás Rua Ó Súilleabháin (1785-1848), the Ivreagh poet and musician, was leaving Caherdaniel, where he had been a teacher, he put all his treasured books on a boat going from Derrynane to Goleen. The boat struck a rock, and sank. After hearing of the fate of his books,

Tomás Rua wrote the song **Amhrán na Leabhar** to the next air.
It is also known as **Cuan Bhéil Inse**.

Amhrán na Leabhar
(The song of the books)

Generally it is better to play the high E notes with the fourth finger on the
A string, particularly in the case of long notes, as in bars 2 and 22.
However, there are occasions when use of the open string results in smoother
bowing, and also allows ornamentation, such as the cut in bar 3.

Go Cuan Bhéil Inse casadh mé, cois Ghóilin aoibhinn Dairbhre
Mar seoltar flít na farraige, thar sáile i gcéin.
I bPortmagee do stadas seal, fé thuairim intinn mhaitheasa
D'fhonn bheith sealad eatarthu, im mháistir léinn.
Is gearr gur chuala an t-eachtra, ag cách, mo léan,
Gur i mbord Eoghain Fhinn do cailleadh theas, an t-árthach tréan
Do phreab mo chroí le h-atuirse, i dtaobh loing an tíosaigh chalma
'S go mb'fearrde an tír í sheasamh seal, ná ráid an tséin.

By Valentia harbour I happened once
Near sweet Goleen Dairbhre
To be the master in Portmagee
Where ships set sail for the ocean deep.
Soon all had the sorrowful story then
Of the sturdy craft, lost at Owen Finn
Sad was my heart for the ship that failed
Better this land had it survived the gale.
(Translation by Tomás Ó Canainn)

The next air is in the key of C, in which the note F is natural. If in doubt about
the positions of the fingers, check the note-chart on page 46. In bars 2 and 14,
the note B is inflected: to play B♭, the first finger is placed near the nut.
Try to use vibrato, on some notes at least. Long notes, like those at the ends
of phrases, are very suitable because they give plenty of time.

An Goirtín Eornan
(The little field of barley)

Aisling Gheal ends on a low D. If this note is played with the fourth finger on the G string, vibrato is possible, but not very easy at the early stages of learning. However, if the note is played on the open string, a vibrato-like effect can be achieved by placing the third finger on the A string, an octave above the open D. Vibrato on this third finger, while the open string is being played, produces a similar kind of result.

Aisling Gheal
(A bright vision)

In bar 12, there are three consecutive notes of the same pitch (A). These can be bowed separately, or can be played in one bow, as indicated. The first and second notes are separated by a cut, and the bow is stopped on the string momentarily to articulate the third note.

Airs, like dance-tunes, are usually played twice or, even occasionally, three times: you should now do likewise. The final air, for the present at least, is well known. Try to include additional ornamentation.

Sliabh na mBan
(The mountain of the women)

Julia Clifford (1914-1997), playing a 'Stroh' fiddle (also known as a 'Phono' fiddle)
Photograph courtesy of the Cork Examiner

10. Putting it all together

One of the hallmarks of the better traditional performer is the ability to decorate a melody spontaneously and with ease, creating music which is exciting and inventive, but yet very much in the traditional idiom. For this, a wide knowledge of the tradition itself is necessary, which as we have already seen, is acquired primarily by listening. Records are excellent sources of music: Appendix C contains a comprehensive discography. In addition, listen to musicians in your locality, and learn from them as much as possible of what is, after all, your own music.

A traditional musician is not consciously aware of the individual ornaments as such: rather do they form an integral part of the music. To help assimilate the ornamentation into your playing, we will go over all the tune-types again. This time, try to concentrate on playing the tune as a reel or jig, etc., thinking more of its overall effect than of the individual ornaments. Do not feel bound by the bowing and decorations indicated. Vary them as you wish, while still retaining the essence of the tune.

The Cordal Jig

Ending on the last note is rather abrupt, and so unless another jig follows, it is usual to finish on the first bar.

END OF TUNE

In this jig, rolls are used to decorate crotchets. The note sequence, and consequently the fingering, is the same as before. The difference is that the roll starts immediately on playing the note. It is sometimes called a SHORT ROLL.

SHORT ROLL

The same symbol (∾) is used.

The Wheels of the World

One of the variations possible in this jig is to replace the first three notes of bar 5 with a roll on a dotted crotchet.

ROLL IN BAR 5

The first half of bar 6 can be played in a similar manner.

Bars 21 and 22 can be played to feature the open D string sounding almost as a drone underneath the principal melody notes.

ALTERNATIVE FOR
BARS 21 AND 22

In bars 13 and 14 of **O'Callaghan's Hornpipe**, it is necessary to cross strings while playing the bowed triplets. This will need some practice to co-ordinate the fingering and the bow-hand, thus ensuring that the notes are clearly heard. You may omit the middle note (E), and play without this ornament.

O'Callaghan's Hornpipe

Unless this is being played for dancers, in which case they will indicate when
to stop, it is better to finish with the first part. Also it is usual, on the repeat of
the tune, to change the lead-in notes.

BARS 16 AND 1
WHEN REPEATING TUNE

The Fairy Queen

In bar 5 of this hornpipe, two successive triplets can be very effective, but not
easy to bow. The note E should be played with the fourth finger.

TRIPLET ORNAMENTS IN BAR 5

It is also possible to give separate bows to all six notes.

On the final note, the open D string can be played to give a double-stopped
octave. Alternatively F♯ on the D string can be played, producing the interval
of a minor sixth.

DOUBLE - STOPPING ON FINAL NOTE

Miss Langford gives an opportunity to try a short roll, played so far only in a jig. It is faster this time, the tune being a reel. Notice the triplet variation in bar 5. Although not quite a treble, it is very similar in bowing, and in the effect produced.

Miss Langford

Bars 9, 11 and 13 all have the same melody, and so contrast is achieved by varying the ornamentation, as indicated. In bar 13, the crotchet (G) has been replaced by two quavers, the first of which is a note lower. This delay in playing the main note (G) adds a sense of anticipation and 'drive' to the music. Over-use of this ornament reduces its effect considerably.

The key in which a tune is played depends on various factors such as its melodic range, and the instrument being used. A piper may play a particular tune in the key of G because it suits the instrument better, whereas a melodeon-player or fiddle-player may prefer to play the same piece in the key of A. If they all play together, then there has to be agreement on one key! It is a good idea to learn some tunes in two keys, so that the fingering and bowing patterns in each can be compared. This also shows the possibilities of ornamentation in one key as against the other, and generally increases flexibility of fingering, and knowledge of the fingerboard.

The next reel is first played in the key of G. In the second part (or turn), there is extensive string-crossing, for which bowing patterns other than those indicated are possible. Traditional musicians frequently refer to the first part as the TUNE, and the second part as the TURN. To 'turn a tune' is to play the second part.

The Red-Haired Lass

A triplet ornament can be played in place of two quavers at the end of bar 8.

TRIPLET ORNAMENT IN BAR 8

In this case, two of the three notes are played with the same finger, and so practice is needed to play the notes in tune, and in time.

The Red-Haired Lass also goes very well in the key of A – it could be said to sound brighter, being in a higher key. However, this is not the only consideration. The effect produced by string-crossing in the key of G is largely missing when played in A. The open strings occur on different notes of the scale, and consequently on different notes of the tune. Also, the ornamentation is not the same. All these factors affect how it sounds in one key as distinct from another. Play in both, to hear the differences. Bowing and ornamentation have not been marked this time, to encourage you to do it yourself!

The Red-Haired Lass

As mentioned earlier, a slow air may not easily fit into a fixed time-signature, because of the phrasing of the melody. Occasionally it may be necessary to use more than one time-signature in the same piece. Examples of this occur in **Caoineadh an Spailpín**, where some bars have five crotchets. Even so, 'written music' cannot really do justice to such pieces, particularly the phrasing and articulation. Listen to a *sean-nós* singer to hear how these tunes should be interpreted.

Notice that the note B is inflected: ensure that the first finger is placed correctly to play it in tune, particularly when flattened. In bars 4 and 11, a roll is indicated on the note F. This is similar to what we have already had, but being less hurried this time, the emphasis is a little different. Remember to use long bow-strokes, and vibrato if possible.

Caoineadh an Spailpín
(The spalpeen's lament)

Although strictly speaking, this air is not in the key of G, it is sometimes said to be 'in G', because this is the final note, and also to some extent, there is a 'feeling' of this key about the piece.

While slides and polkas may at times appear to have deceptively simple melody lines, they can often give great scope for melodic inventiveness. When the characteristic rhythm is present, this can result in very exciting music. This slide is a good illustration, particularly the last two bars.

Denis Murphy's Slide (2)

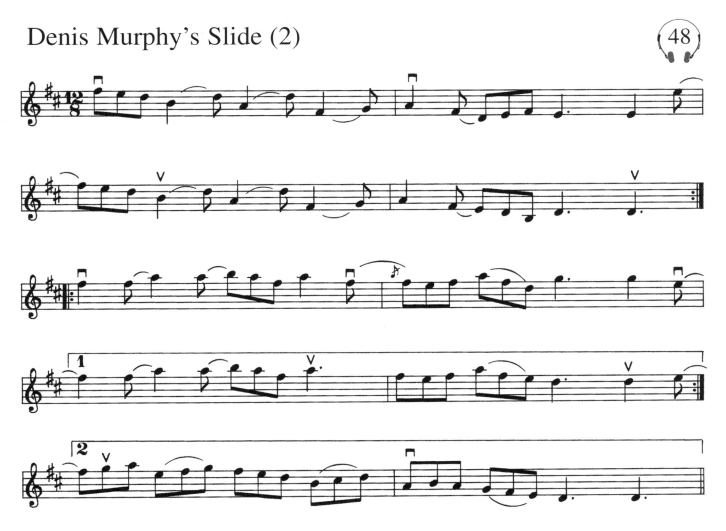

When the tune is being repeated, it is usual to play a high G instead of D at the end of the last bar. This serves as a lead-in to the beginning.

LAST BAR WHEN REPEATING TUNE

When finishing, play the tune as written, with a down bow on the last note.

Among the points to notice in **The Dark Girl** is the roll in bar 10, which is played as near to the end of the note as possible. Listen also for the DRONE-BOWING. This is a type of double-stopping in which an open string is bowed along (as if incidentally) with the melody. In playing polkas, it is very effective, particularly on the 'off-beat', because it emphasizes the rhythm. The effect is diminished greatly if the bowing is exaggerated: it needs to be subtle. Again this time, the melody line is highly ornate, especially in the second half of each part.

The Dark Girl 49

Ornamentation generally involves the playing of additional notes in order to decorate the melody line. Occasionally, the opposite has an equally good effect, when a group of notes is replaced by a LONG NOTE. In bar 17 of the next jig, a long E may be played instead of the first three notes.

LONG NOTE IN BAR 17

A double-stop on a long note gives added emphasis. In particular, when the note is an open string, a unison double-stop is effective.

UNISON DOUBLE-STOP in BAR 17

If the third finger, rather than the fourth, is used to slide from D up to E,
it will need to be back in time to play the next note in tune.

Bowing and ornamentation, being no longer indicated, are at your own discretion.

The Cliffs of Moher

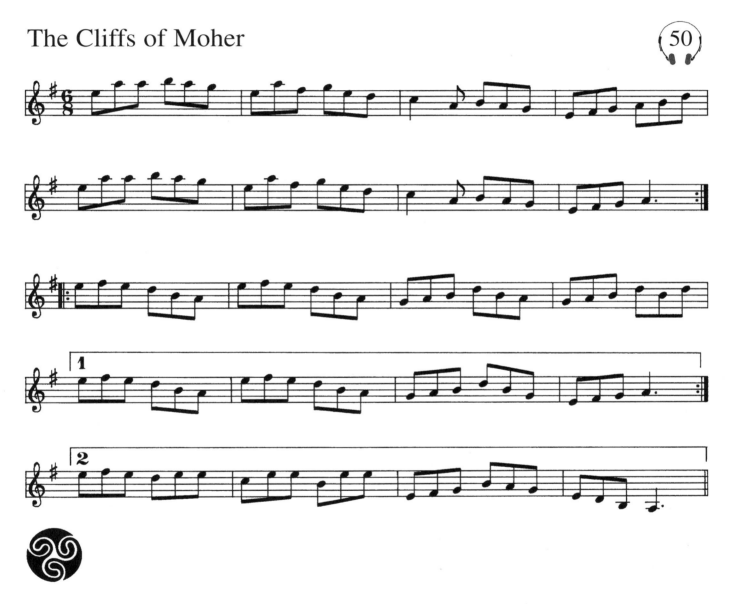

With very few exceptions, traditional tunes have a musical range which lies
between the low G string and B on the E string. Thus they are played with the
hand in the FIRST POSITION. Rarely is it necessary to stretch the fourth finger,
or move the hand up the neck to another position to reach a higher note.
Many tunes have a range of one and a half octaves or less, and can be played
on three strings, or perhaps two. A smaller number have a range of over two
octaves, and use all four strings. The last jig was one of these, as is this reel,
a firm favourite with fiddle-players.

Doctor Gilbert

In common with the other instruments used in traditional music, there are different styles of playing the fiddle. As used in this context, the term STYLE means either the way in which one musician plays, as distinct from another, or alternatively, the distinguishing features of playing which identify musicians from a particular area. In the past before the era of mass-communication, styles of playing were confined largely to their own geographic regions. However since music in all styles has now become more available to everyone, through recordings, radio and television, regional styles are no longer confined to their own areas, and the boundaries between them less obvious.

As stated earlier, traditional music is based primarily on a single melodic line, and relies for much of its effect on the ornamentation, or decoration, of the melody. Ornaments such as the 'roll', 'treble', 'cut' and 'double cut' form an intrinsic part of fiddle-playing. Their effect can often be rhythmic as much as melodic, depending on the interpretation of the player and on the emphasis given in each particular case. Also, bowing is a fundamental feature of playing, and has a significant influence on the sound produced by the fiddle. The bow is used to accentuate certain notes, and to create the appropriate rhythmic articulation, or swing, especially in the case of dance music. The extent to which the different kinds of ornamentation are used, and the various ways in which the bow can create distinctive rhythmic nuances and colour, vary from player to player, and from one style of playing to another. Repertoire can also be considered to be an element of style, in the sense that specific types of tunes and dance-rhythms may feature more prominently in particular regions. And of course, the personality of the musician contributes a great deal to the creative process, and so has a major influence on the style of playing.

The principal regional styles are those of DONEGAL, SLIGO, CLARE and SLIABH LUACHRA. It is impossible to be definite in listing all the features of each regional style, because not all musicians in a particular region play the same way. Even within each region, there may be noticeable differences from one area to another. It is difficult to define the boundaries of each region, to say where one style stops and another starts. Indeed, it may well be more satisfactory to consider a gradual change of style (perhaps abrupt in places) on an axis stretching from Sliabh Luachra in the south to Donegal in the north – in essence, a continuum of playing styles along this line. It is probably not without significance that these are situated in the west of the country, close to Gaeltacht areas. In considering regional styles of playing, the analogy with spoken language may be helpful. Speakers in a particular dialect will not all speak in exactly the same way with identical accents and vocabulary. However, their speech will have many characteristics in common, and be recognisable as being the 'language' of a particular dialect and geographic area.

Donegal fiddle-playing is characterised by single-note bowing, with short bow-strokes. Ornamentation is achieved primarily with the bow-hand, trebling being used to a much greater extent than rolls. The tempo is generally fast, thus contributing to the overall staccato-like effect of this style. To hear how it sounds, listen to the playing of one of its finest exponents, John Doherty (1894-1977): his recordings provide an excellent insight into this style of play-ing. The musical repertoire of the region includes tunes not usually played elsewhere, such as highlands and strathspeys. The connection, musically and otherwise, with Scotland is very evident in these titles.

Moving down to Sligo, the pace is still fast, and the playing very rhythmic. Rolls as well as trebles are used, and the bowing is smoother. The fiddle-music of this region is more widely known than any other, mainly because of the recordings of Michael Coleman (1891-1945), James Morrison (1893-1947) and Paddy Killoran (1904-1965), all of whom had emigrated from Co. Sligo to New York. Their individual musical output on record (78 RPM) during the 1920s, '30s and '40s was both compelling and prolific: Coleman made at least eighty recordings. Many of these records were sent home to Ireland, and became in effect the 'standard' to which fiddle-players all over the country aspired. Michael Coleman in particular, with technical brilliance allied to his musical creativity, has been a source of inspiration not only for fiddle-players, but for many other musicians. His settings of tunes, such as **Bonnie Kate** and **Jenny's Chickens**, have become classics, and feature in the repertoire of almost all traditional musicians.

The huge impact of Coleman's playing was well summarised by fiddle-player Patrick Kelly of Cree, Co Clare, when he is supposed to have said: "The worst thing that ever happened to the West Clare style of fiddling was the appearance of Michael Coleman's records." In Clare, the tempo is slower, thus allowing the player to concentrate more on the melodic features of the music. Extensive use is made of left-hand ornamentation, such as the roll, coupled with long fluid bow-strokes. A distinction is often made between the style of west Clare and that of east Clare. The former is well represented by the fine playing of Bobby Casey (1926-2000), and the latter by Paddy Canny (b. 1919), whose wonderful music has had an influence on many, even those who play in other styles.

Sliabh Luachra (The Mountain of Rushes), situated on the Cork/Kerry border along the upper reaches of the river Blackwater, is renowned for slides and polkas. The direct, rhythmic style of playing these has permeated to the other dance tunes. As the music is frequently played for the dancing of sets, it is lively and exuberant. Ornamentation is achieved mainly with the left hand, and the bow-hand provides the characteristic rhythm and swing. A particular feature is the use of open strings to provide a drone-effect. And it is not uncommon, when two or more are playing, that the tune is played an octave lower by one of the musicians. This is sometimes called 'playing the bass', and is also to be found in the Donegal tradition. The records of Pádraig O'Keeffe (1887-1963), Denis Murphy (1910-1974) and Julia Clifford (1914-1997) all contain superb examples of this style of music. To a greater extent than in the other regions, the repertoire of players here generally includes a number of slow airs, such as that great tune, **Caoineadh Uí Dhómhnaill** (O'Donnell's Lament).

Of course there are some players whose music may not belong to a particular regional style, and so do not fit comfortably into the general classification just described. For example, Tommy Potts (1912-1988), a native of Dublin, played music in a highly personal way with a distinctly individual style. His unusual versions of tunes, and unique interpretation, included influences, not only from within the tradition but from outside as well. Seán McGuire (b. 1924) plays in a flamboyant virtuoso style that has many of the Sligo characteristics and much of its repertoire, but is uniquely different at the same time. Even though his music is often controversial, he has had a major influence on many fiddle-players, because of the exceptional quality of his playing. Paddy Cronin (b. 1925), who was a pupil of Pádraig O'Keeffe, spent about forty years living in Boston. His distinctive music has elements of both the Sliabh Luachra style, which he learned at home, and the Sligo style, which was more prevalent in the United States during his time there.

Fiddle-players, like other musicians, are generally influenced by those whose playing they most admire. Before the advent of mass-communication, this usually meant local players, or perhaps a travelling fiddle master. However with increased ease of travel and the widespread availability of recorded music on CD, as well as on radio and television, sources of influence are no longer confined to the same locality. These factors have led, throughout the last quarter of the twentieth century, to the creation of individual or personal styles of playing, in which elements from some or all of the regional styles are included. The result is a way of playing which is immediately recognisable as being that of a particular musician. Fiddle-players such as Kevin Burke, Liz Carroll, John Carty, Séamus Connolly, Séamus Creagh, Frankie Gavin, Paddy Glackin, Martin Hayes, Seán Keane, James Kelly, Brendan McGlinchey, Connie O'Connell, Tommy Peoples, and many, many more all have very distinctive styles of playing: yet, regional influences are clearly evident.

In developing your own style of playing, particularly when learning at first, it is often helpful to copy the playing of some one whose music is readily available, perhaps on a recording. This should not be continued longer than is necessary. As stated earlier, it is a good idea to listen to musicians in your own locality, and to learn from them as much as possible of what is, in effect, your own music. However, slavish imitation of another's playing clearly diminishes the scope for musical creativity and self-expression, ultimately leading to a standardization of playing styles. An essential feature of the music is thereby lost.

Before playing **Lucy Campbell**, the final tune in this section of the book, here is a story about a fiddle-player of previous times, one of the countless number of musicians to whom we are indebted for the music we enjoy so much today.

THE HARD TACK

'All the others (airs) were written from memory by one John Daly, who gave me my first violin lessons in February, 1872. At that time, as well as I can remember, Daly was about 60 years of age. He was said to have been a farmer's son in the Co. Cork, that he could have succeeded to the farm, but he preferred the life of a wandering minstrel. He often told us he had heard the great Paganini in Cork. He was a man of most refined nature, spoke with a nice accent, and was most particular about his grammar and pronunciation. He played for the dances of the gentry, the farmers and the labourers in the counties of Tipperary, Waterford and Kilkenny: his fee was collected in a hat that went the round of the company. His teaching fee was sixpence per lesson, and a glass of punch. When the tune slipped his memory for the time being, a sip or two of punch brought it back in marvellously quick time. He made fiddles, of Irish wood, which retailed at half a crown each, and far back in memory there is an impression that he nailed tacks into the finger board, as guides (painful sometimes) for the places of the fingers.'

P. J. Griffith to Joyce, February 14, 1902.
Reprinted from Ceol : Vol. 2, No. 4.

Lucy Campbell

Appendix A (page 125) contains a selection of 101 tunes, some of which are popular and widely played, others not as well known. All the different rhythms, as well as airs, are included. Since traditional music is subject to continuous change and variation (in a word, IMPROVISATION) as it is passed from one player to another, there is no 'one exact' version of any tune. Even if versions are very similar, they are never identical. Those given are 'fiddle versions', in the sense that they are played by fiddle-players, and are well suited to the instrument. To improve and develop your playing further, and at the same time add to your repertoire, learn these tunes, although not necessarily in the order in which they are written. A large number of them, arranged and played in sets as would normally be done by traditional musicians, feature on two specially prepared recordings. Refer to page 127 for more detailed information.

As stated earlier, the melodic shape of a large number of tunes has been influenced greatly by the fiddle: this is so because traditional music is composed primarily on the instrument itself. Tunes are being varied continuously as they pass from one player to another, and from instrument to instrument. To a certain extent, this makes all traditional musicians part-composers as well, although they would not consider this to be the case. The large collection of tunes we have today owes much to generations of anonymous but gifted musicians, many of whom were fiddle-players. In addition, a number of fiddle-players, among them Ed Reavy (1898-1988), Joe Liddy (1904-1992), Seán Ryan (1919-1985), Paddy Fahy (b. 1926) and Charlie Lennon (b. 1938), have each composed a large number of tunes that are in wide circulation as part of the living tradition. The music of these composers is included in the repertoire of almost all traditional musicians, especially fiddle-players. Many of these tunes have been assimilated so well into the tradition that they are generally regarded as 'old' tunes rather than the relatively recent compositions which they are: this attribute is considered to be one of the characteristics of a good tune. Appendix B (page 173) lists a number of collections of tunes, as well as other publications in which additional information on traditional music and fiddle-playing may be obtained.

The discography in Appendix C (page 175) contains an extensive list of recorded fiddle-music, including not only 'solo' and 'compilation' recordings, but also those of duets and trios, in which the fiddle is featured. These recordings serve as a useful source for learning new repertoire, for hearing various styles of playing, and of course for some very good music. Perhaps one day, your CD will also be included here.

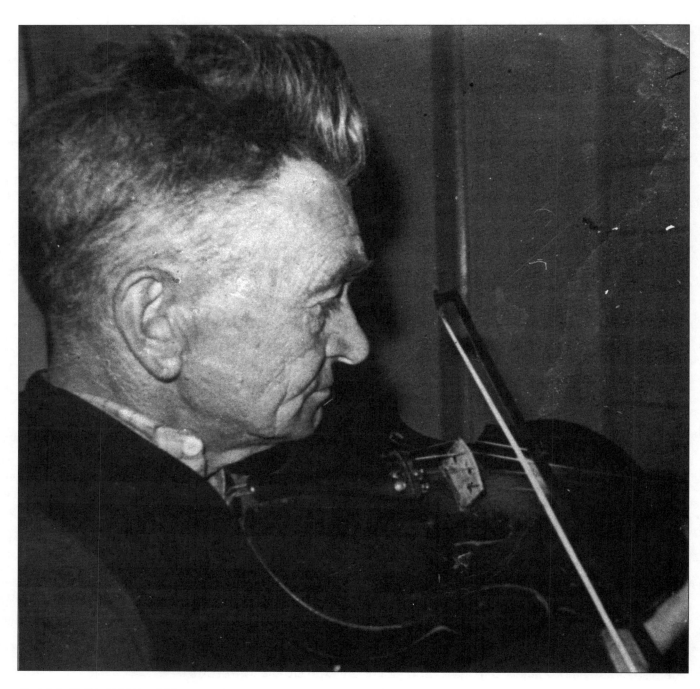

Patrick Kelly (1905-1976)
Photograph taken by Seán Keane & supplied by Mick O'Connor

Appendix A – 101 Selected Tunes

DOUBLE JIGS

	No.		No.
Banks of Lough Gowna, The	8	Luck Penny, The	9
Brennan's Favourite	19	Merry Old Woman, The	10
Connie O'Connell's Jig	3	Munster Buttermilk	16
Eavesdropper, The	5	Petticoat Loose	14
Father O'Flynn	2	Price of My Pig, The	7
Frost is All Over, The	4	Sporting Pitchfork, The	18
Geese in the Bog, The	6	Tell Her I Am	15
Gullane Jig, The	11	Tripping Up the Stairs	1
Humours of Lisheen, The	12	Up and About in the Morning	13
Irish Giant, The	17	Willie Coleman's Jig	20

SLIDES

	No.		No.
Cuil Aodha Slide, The	27	Johnny Murphy's Slide	23
Dan O'Keeffe's Slide	26	Michael Murphy's Slide	24
Danny Ab's Slide	25	Nell O'Sullivan's Slide	28
Dingle Regatta	21	Pádraig O'Keeffe's Slide	30
Glountane Slide, The	22	Toormore Slide, The	29

SLIP JIGS

	No.		No.
Boy's of Ballysodare, The	33	Hardiman the Fiddler	31
Foxhunter's Jig, The	34	Port an Deoraí	32

POLKAS

	No.		No.
Ballydesmond Polka, The	36	Knocknaboul Polka, The (2)	50
Blue Ribbon, The	44	Matt Teehan's Polka	41
Cappamore Polka, The	40	Maurice Manley's Polka	35
Dan Coakley's Polka	42	Mick Duggan's Polka (1)	45
Din Tarrant's Polka (1)	37	Mick Duggan's Polka (2)	46
Din Tarrant's Polka (2)	38	Mick Duggan's Polka (3)	47
Farewell to Whiskey	48	New Roundabout, The	39
Knocknaboul Polka, The (1)	49	Pádraig O'Keeffe's Polka	43

REELS

HORNPIPES

SET DANCES

AIRS

A large number of these tunes, arranged and played in sets as would normally be done by traditional musicians, feature on two specially prepared recordings. Additional instrumentation and accompaniment are provided on various tracks by Dave Hennessy (melodeon), Eoin Ó Riabhaigh (uilleann pipes), Bríd Cranitch (piano and harpsichord), Mick Daly (guitar), Colm Murphy (bodhrán), Tom Stephens (guitar).

TAKE A BOW, Ossian OSSCD 5

1. The Providence Reel/The Pigeon the Gate/The Killavil Reel.
2. The Knocknaboul Polkas.
3. The Cúil Aodha Slide/Dingle Regatta/The Gleanntán Slide.
4. Táimse im Chodladh.
5. The Luck Penny/The Merry Old Woman.
6. The Stack of Wheat/The Galway Hornpipe.
7. The Broken Pledge/The Crib of Perches.
8. Madam Bonaparte.
9. Lord Gordon.
10. Tripping up the Stairs/Father O'Flynn.
11. Maurice Manley's Polka/The Ballydesmond Polka/Dan Coakley's Polka.
12. Na Connerys.
13. The Price of my Pig/The Tullagh Reel.
14. Danny Ab's Slide/Dan O'Keeffe's Slide.
15. The Boys of Ballysodare/The New Policeman/The Boys of Malin/The High Road to Linton/ The Monsignor's Blessing/The Wild Irishman.

GIVE IT SHTICK, Ossian OSSCD 6

1. Tell Her I Am/Munster Buttermilk.
2. Pretty Maggie Morrissey/Higgin's Hornpipe/Walsh's Hornpipe.
3. The Bunch of Keys.
4. Johnny Murphy's Slide/ Michael Murphy's Slide.
5. An Buachaill Caol Dubh.
6. Mick Duggan's Polkas.
7. The Foxhunter's Jig/Eileen O'Callaghan's Reel/The Bantry Lasses/The Maid Behind the Bar.
8. Connie O'Connell's Jig/The Frost Is All Over.
9. The Blackbird.
10. The Sligo Maid/The Congress.
11. Port an Deoraí.
12. Henry McDermott Roe.
13. The Banks of Lough Gowna/Willie Coleman's Jig/Brennan's Favourite.
14. Din Tarrant's Polkas.
15. Master Crowley/The Roscommon Reel.

These recordings may be ordered directly from
Ossian Publications Ltd., c/o Music Sales Limited
Newmarket Road, Bury St Edmunds, Suffolk, Great Britain

Paddy Canny (b. 1919)
Photograph courtesy of Tony C. Kearns

Double Jigs

1. Tripping up the Stairs

2. Father O'Flynn

3. Connie O'Connell's Jig

4. The Frost is all over

5. The Eavesdropper

6. The Geese in the Bog

7. The Price of my Pig

8. The Banks of Lough Gowna

9. The Lucky Penny

10. The Merry Old Woman

11. The Gullane Jig

12. The Humours of Lisheen

13. Up and About in the Morning

14. Petticoat Loose

15. Tell her I am

16. Munster Buttermilk

17. The Irish Giant

18. The Sporting Pitchfork

19. Brennan's Favourite

20. Willie Coleman's Jig

Slides

21. The Dingle Regatta

22. The Gleanntán Slide

23. Johnny Murphy's Slide

24. Michael Murphy's Slide

25. Danny Ab's Slide

26. Dan O'Keeffe's Slide

27. The Cúil Aodha Slide

28. Nell O'Sullivan's Slide

29. The Toormore Slide

30. Pádraig O'Keeffe's Slide

Slip Jigs

31. Hardiman the Fiddler

32. Port an Deoraí

33. The Boys of Ballysodare

34. The Foxhunter's Jig

Polkas

35. Maurice Manley's Polka

36. The Ballydesmond Polka

37. Din Tarrant's Polka (1)

38. Din Tarrant's Polka (2)

39. The New Roundabout

40. The Cappamore Polka

41. Matt Teehan's Polka

42. Dan Coakley's Polka

43. Pádraig O'Keeffe's Polka

44. The Blue Ribbon

45. Mick Duggan's Polka (1)

46. Mick Duggan's Polka (2)

47. Mick Duggan's Polka (3)

48. Farewell to Whiskey

49. The Knocknaboul Polka (1)

50. The Knocknaboul Polka (2)

Reels

51. The Providence Reel

52. The Wise Maid

53. The Sligo Maid

54. The Congress

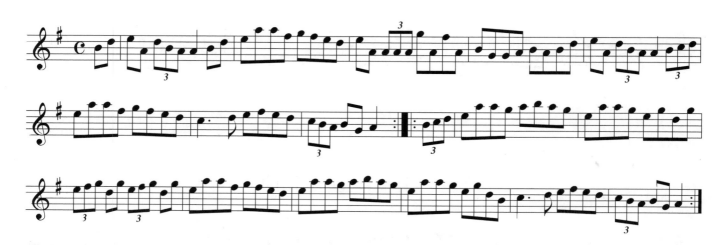

55. Dinny O'Brien's Reel

56. Eileen O'Callaghan's Reel

57. The Pigeon on the Gate

58. The Killavil Reel

59. Far from Home

60. The Volunteer

61. The Boys of Malin

62. The High Road to Linton

63. The Monsignor's Blessing

64. The Wild Irishman

65. Andy McGann's Reel

66. The Humours of Scariff

67. The Maid behind the Bar

68. Paddy Ryan's Dream

69. The Crib of Perches

70. The Broken Pledge

71. Master Crowley

72. The Roscommon Reel

73. All Hands Around

74. The Bantry Lasses

75. O'Dowd's Favourite

76. Sean Reid's Reel

77. The Tullagh Reel

78. The New Policeman

79. Rattigan's Reel

80. The Bunch of Keys

81. Jenny's Welcome to Charlie

82. Lord Gordon

Hornpipes

83. Pretty Maggie Morrissey

84. Fallon's Hornpipe

85. Ballymanus Fair

86. The Stack of Wheat

87. The Galway Hornpipe

88. Father Dollard's Hornpipe

89. Higgins' Hornpipe

90. Walsh's Hornpipe

91. Cross the Fence

Set Dances

92. The Job of Journeywork

93. Madam Bonaparte

94. The Blackbird

95. Saint Patrick's Day

Airs

96. An Buachaill Caol Dubh

97. Táimse im' Choladh

98. Na Connerys

99. A' Raibh Tú ag an gCarraig?

100. Pléaráca na Ruarcach

101. Henry McDermott Roe

Bobby Casey (1926-2000)
Photograph courtesy of Tony C. Kearns

Appendix B - Bibliography

COLLECTIONS OF TUNES

Breathnach, Breandán, *Ceol Rince Na hÉireann – Vol. 1*. An Gúm, Dublin, 1963.

Breathnach, Breandán, *Ceol Rince Na hÉireann – Vol. 2*. An Gúm, Dublin, 1976.

Breathnach, Breandán, *Ceol Rince Na hÉireann – Vol. 3*. An Gúm, Dublin, 1985.

Breathnach, Breandán, (ed. Jackie Small), *Ceol Rince Na hÉireann - Vol. 4*. An Gúm, Dublin, 1996.

Breathnach, Breandán, (ed. Jackie Small), *Ceol Rince Na hÉireann - Vol. 5*. An Gúm, Dublin, 1999.

Lennon, Charlie, Musical Memories – *Traditional Irish Music Vol. 1*. Worldmusic Publications, Dublin, 1993.

Liddy, Joe, *The Leitrim Fiddler*. Comhaltas Ceoltóirí Éireann, Dublin, 1981.

Liddy, Joe, *The Leitrim Fiddler – Vol. 2*. Comhaltas Ceoltóirí Éireann, Dublin, 1991.

Moylan, Terry (ed.), *Johnny O'Leary of Sliabh Luachra* (Dance Music from the Cork-Kerry Border). Lilliput Press, Dublin, 1994.

Ó Canainn, Tomás, *Traditional Slow Airs of Ireland*. Ossian Publications, Cork, 1995.

O'Neill, Francis, *The Dance Music of Ireland*. Waltons, Dublin, 1965. (First published by Lyon & Healy, Chicago, 1907).

O'Sullivan, Dónal, *Carolan, The Life Times and Music of an Irish Harper*. Ossian Publications, Cork, 2001. (First published by Routledge and Kegan Paul, London, 1958).

Reavy, Joseph M., *The Collected Compositions of Ed Reavy*. Green Grass Music, Drumshanbo, Co. Leitrim, 1995.

Ryan, Seán, *The Hidden Ireland*. Ryan Family, Mountmellick, Co. Laois, 1994.

Roche, Francis, *The Roche Collection of Traditional Irish Music*. Ossian Publications, Cork, 1982. (First published by McCullough Pigott, Dublin, 1927).

FURTHER READING

Breathnach, Breandán, *Folk Music and Dances of Ireland*. Ossian Publications, Cork, 1996. (First published by Mercier Press, 1971).

Carolan, Nicholas, *A Short Discography of Irish Folk Music*. Folk Music Society of Ireland, Dublin, 1987.

De Marco, Tony, and Miles Krassen, *A Trip to Sligo* (A guide to the Sligo style). Silver Spear Publications, Pittsburgh, Pennsylvania, 1978.

Feldman, Allen, and Eamonn O'Doherty, *The Northern Fiddler*. Oak Publications, London, 1985. (First published by Blackstaff Press, Belfast, 1979).

Lyth, David, *Bowing Styles in Irish Fiddle Playing – Vol. 1*. Comhaltas Ceoltóirí Éireann, Dublin, 1981.

Lyth, David, *Bowing Styles in Irish Fiddle Playing – Vol. 2*. Comhaltas Ceoltóirí Éireann, Dublin, 1996.

Mac Aoidh, Caoimhín, *Between the Jigs and the Reels* (The Donegal Fiddle Tradition). Drumlin Publications, Co. Leitrim, 1994.

Ó Canainn, Tomás, *Traditional Music in Ireland*. Ossian Publications, Cork, 1993. (First published by Routledge & Kegan Paul. London 1978.).

Ó hAllmhuráin, Gearóid, *A Pocket History of Irish Traditional Music*. The O'Brien Press, Dublin, 1998.

Vallely, F. (ed.), *The Companion to Traditional Irish Music*. Cork University Press, Cork, 1999.

Ward, Alan, *Music from Sliabh Luachra*. Topic Records, London, 1976.

Appendix C - Discography

This discography of fiddle music includes not only 'solo' and 'compilation' recordings, but also those of duets and trios, in which the fiddle is featured. In the case of these entries, the names of the other musicians are given in parentheses. The instruments used with the fiddle in such combinations are accordion/melodeon, flute, uilleann pipes, concertina, harmonica and banjo, as well as the fiddle itself. Many of the recordings include accompaniment on piano, guitar, bouzouki and occasionally bodhrán.

For each entry, the title of the recording is followed by the label (the name of the record company) and the number of the recording. Although there is no standard numbering system in use, records are generally identified by an alphanumeric 'number', one containing both letters and numbers. The designation 'CD' in the number denotes that it is on compact-disc, as well as being on cassette tape and, in the case of older recordings, on vinyl long-playing record (LP). A number without this designation usually, but not always, indicates that it is not on CD, but on cassette or LP, or both. When trying to locate a particular recording, it is best to know the name of the musician(s), the record label and the numeric part of the number.

Not all the recordings listed may be available commercially as a result of deletion by various record companies. However, because of their importance, they feature in specialist collections and record libraries, and so are included. A small number have been issued on two labels, either because they have been deleted from the first, in which case they are re-issues, or because of a licencing agreement between two labels to cover different countries. Details concerning both labels are given in these cases.

Breatnach, Máire,
> *Branohm – The Voyage of Bran*, Celtic Heartbeat UD 53094.
> *Celtic Lovers*, Hummingbird Records HBCD 0013.
> *Angels' Candles – Coinnle na nAingeal*, MB Cala 101 CD.

Burke, Kevin
> *If the Cap Fits*, Mulligan LUNCD 021; Green Linnet GLCD 3009.
> *Sweeney's Dream*, Folkways FW 8876; Ossian OSSCD 18.
> *Promenade* (with Mícheál Ó Domhnaill), Mulligan LUNCD 028; Green Linnet GLCD 3010.
> *Eavesdropper* (with Jackie Daly), Mulligan LUNCD 039; Green Linnet GLCD 3002.
> *Portland* (with Mícheál Ó Domhnaill), Green Linnet GLCD 1041.
> *Up Close*, Green Linnet GLCD 1052.

The Celtic Fiddle Festival (with Johnny Cunningham and Christian Lemaitre), Green Linnet GLCD 1133.

Encore (with Johnny Cunningham and Christian Lemaitre), Green Linnet GLCD 1189.

In Concert, Green Linnet GLCD 1196.

Bradley, Paul

Atlantic Roar, Outlet PTICD 1090.

Byrne, Francie and Mickey

Ceol na dTéad, Cló Iar-Chonnachta CIC 078.

Byrne, James

The Road to Glenlough, Claddagh CC52CD.

Byrnes, Martin

Martin Byrnes, Leader LEA 2004.

Canny, Paddy

Traditional Music from the Legendary East Clare Fiddler, Cló Iar Chonnachta CICD129.

Canny, Paddy, and P. J. Hayes

All Ireland Champions, Dublin DU-LP 1003.

Carroll, Liz

Kiss Me Kate (with Tommy Maguire), Shanachie 34012.

A Friend Indeed, Shanachie SHCD 34013.

Liz Carroll, Green Linnet GLCD 1092.

Trian (with Billy McComiskey and Daithí Sproule), Flying Fish FF 70586.

Trian II (with Billy McComiskey and Daithí Sproule), Green Linnet GLCD 1159.

Lost in the Loop, Green Linnet GLCD 1199.

Carty, John

Last Night's Fun, Shanachie 79098.

Yeh, that's all it is, Shanachie 78034.

Casey, Bobby,

Taking Flight, Mulligan LUN 018;

Casey in the Cowhouse, Bellbridge 001.

Casey, Nollaig

Lead the Knave (with Arty McGlynn), Round Tower MCGCD 1.

Clifford, Julia

The Star of Munster Trio (with John Clifford and Billy Clifford), Topic 12TS310;   Ossian OSS 45.

The Humours of Lisheen (with John Clifford), Topic 12TS311; Ossian OSS 14.

Ceol as Sliabh Luachra (with Billy Clifford), Gael-Linn CEFC 092.

Coleman, Michael

The Legacy of Michael Coleman, Shanachie 33002.

The Classic Recordings of Michael Coleman, Shanachie 33006.

Michael Coleman 1891-1945, Gael-Linn/Viva Voce CEFCD 161 (2 CDs with book).

Collins, Kathleen.

Traditional Music of Ireland, Shanachie 34010.

Connolly, Séamus.

The Banks of the Shannon (with Paddy O'Brien and Charlie Lennon), Comhaltas CLCD 40.

Notes from my Mind, Green Linnet GLCD 1087.

Here and There, Green Linnet GLCD 1098.

Warming Up (with Martin Mulhare and Jack Coen), Green Linnet GLCD 1135.

Conway, Brian, and Tony DeMarco

The Apple in Winter, Green Linnet CSIF 1035.

Cooper, Pete

The Wounded Hussar, Fiddling from Scratch CDFFS 002.

Cranitch, Matt

Any Old Time (with Dave Hennessy and Mick Daly), Mulligan LUN 047.

Éistigh Seal, Gael-Linn CEFC 104.

Phoenix (with Dave Hennessy and Mick Daly), Dara DARACD 025.

Take a Bow, Ossian OSSCD 5.

Give it Shtick, Ossian OSSCD 6.

Crossing (with Dave Hennessy and Mick Daly), Dara DARACD 072.

Sliabh Notes (with Dónal Murphy and Tommy O'Sullivan), Cross Border Media CBMCD 018; Kells Music KM-9506.

Gleanntán (with Dónal Murphy and Tommy O'Sullivan), Ossian OSSCD 114.

Creagh, Séamus

Jackie Daly and Séamus Creagh, Gael-Linn CEFCD 057.

Came the Dawn, Ossian OSSCD 90.

Séamus Creagh and Aidan Coffey, Ossian OSSCD 112.

Cronin, Johnny

Johnny Cronin and Joe Burke, Shanachie 29005.

Cronin, Paddy

Kerry's Own, Outlet OAS 3002.

Cullen, Noreen

Bow Bridges, Celtic Music CMCD063.

Custy, Mary

With a Lot of Help from their Friends (with Eoin O'Neill), Celtic Music CMC 064.

The Ways of the World (with Eoin O'Neill), Celtic Music CMCD 065.

After 10.30 (with Stephen Flaherty), own label MCCD004.

Custy, Tola

Setting Free (with Cyril O'Donoghue), Cló Iar-Chonnachta CICD 098.

Doherty, John

John Doherty, Comhaltas CL 10.

Bundle and Go, Topic 12TS398; Ossian OSSCD 17.

Taisce – The Celebrated Recordings, Gael-Linn CEFCD 072.

Doherty, Liz

Last Orders, Foot Stompin' Records CDFSR1702.

Doherty, Mickey

The Gravel Walks, Cumann Béaloideas Éireann CBE 002.

Dolan, Pakie

The Forgotten Fiddle Player of the 1920s, Viva Voce 006CD.

Donnelly, Des

Remember Des Donnelly, 'own label' DDCD001.

Donnelly, Dezi

Familiar Footsteps, 'own label' DD9901.

Duffy, Johnny

Memories of Sligo (with Tommy Healy), Topic 12TS335; Ossian OSS 46.

Duffy, Philip

Coleman's Cross, GTD Heritage HC 030.

Real to Reel, GTD Heritage HC 107.

Fahy, Máirín

Máirín, Radio Telefís Éireann TORTECD 232.

Farr, Lucy

Heart and Home, Veteran Tapes VT 123.

Folan, Declan

Skin and Bow, Sound Records SUNCD23.

Furey, Ted

Toss the Feathers, Outlet PTICD 1020.

Gavin, Frankie

Frankie Gavin and Alec Finn, Shanachie SHCD 34009.

Ómós do Joe Cooley (with Paul Brock), Gael-Linn CEFCD 115.

Frankie Goes to Town, Bee's Knees BKCD 001; Green Linnet GLCD 3051.

An Irish Christmas, Bee's Knees BKCD 003.

Irlande (with Aidan Coffey and Arty McGlynn), Ocora OC 560021CD.

Best of Frankie Gavin, Radio Telefís Éireann RTECD 187.

Gillespie, Hugh

Classic Recordings of Irish Traditional Fiddle Music, Topic 12T364; Green Linnet GLCD 3066.

Glackin, Kevin and Séamus

Na Saighneáin - Northern Lights, Gael-Linn CEFCD 140.

Glackin, Paddy

Glackin, Gael-Linn CEFC 060.

Doublin' (with Paddy Keenan), Tara Music TARACD 2007.

Hidden Ground (with Jolyon Jackson), Tara Music TARA 2009.

The Flags of Dublin (with Mick Gavin and Michael O'Brien), Topic 12TS383; Ossian OSS 31.

Rabharta Ceoil - In Full Spate, Gael-Linn CEFCD 153.

Séideán Sí (with Robbie Hannan), Gael-Linn CEFCD 171.

Reprise – Athchuairt (with Mícheál Ó Domhnaill), Gael-Linn CEFCD180.

Griffin, Vincent

Traditional Fiddle Music from County Clare, Topic 12TS383; Ossian OSS 73.

Traditional Irish Fiddle Music, own label AYLECD 001.

Harrington, Gerry

Scéal Eile (with Eoghan O'Sullivan), Mulligan LUNCD 059.

The New Road (with Charlie Piggott), Cló Iar-Chonnachta CICD 142.

Hayden, Cathal

Handed Down, Rainbow RBC 116.

Cathal Hayden, Cross Border Media CBMCD 012.

Cathal Hayden, 'own label' HOOK001.

Hayes, Martin

Martin Hayes, Green Linnet GLCD 1127.

Under the Moon, Green Linnet GLCD 1155.

The Lonesome Touch (with Denis Cahill), Green Linnet GLCD 1181.

Live in Seattle (with Denis Cahill), Green Linnet GLCD 1195.

Horan, Séamus

Music from County Leitrim (with Packie Duignan), Topic 12TS339; Ossian OSS 75.

Ivers, Eileen

Fresh Takes (with John Whelan), Green Linnet GLCD 1075.

Eileen Ivers, Green Linnet GLCD 1139.

Wild Blue, Green Linnet GLCD 1166.

Keane, Seán

Gusty's Frolics, Claddagh CC17CD.

Seán Keane, Ogham BLB 5005.

Contentment is Wealth (with Matt Molloy), Green Linnet GLCD 1058.

Jig it in Style, Claddagh CCF25CD.

The Fire Aflame (with Matt Molloy and Liam O'Flynn), Claddagh CCF30CD.

Keegan, Josephine

Irish Traditional Music, Outlet COAS 3030.

Kelly, James

Capel Street, Bowhand Records BOW 0001.

Traditional Music of Ireland (with Paddy O'Brien and Daithí Sproule), Shanachie 34014.

The Ring Sessions (with Zan McLeod), Phaeton SPINCD 999.

Traditional Irish Music, Capelhouse (no catalogue number).

Kelly, John

Fiddle and Concertina Player, Topic 12TFRS504.

Kelly, John (Jnr) and James

John and James Kelly – Irish Traditional Fiddle Music, Tara Music TARA 1008; Outlet PTICD 1041.

Killoran, Paddy

Paddy Killoran's Back in Town, Shanachie 33003.

Larrissey, Brendan

A Flick of the Wrist, Cross Border Media CBMCD 016.

Up the Moy Road, own label BLMC01.

Lennon, Ben

The Natural Bridge, Cló Iar-Chonnachta CICD139.

Lennon, Charlie

Deora an Deoraí, Gael-Linn CEFC 112.

Lucky in Love (with Mick O'Connor), Comhaltas CL 22.

Musical Memories, Worldmusic Publications WOMCD 101.

Linnane, Tony

Noel Hill and Tony Linnane, Tara Music TARACD 2006.

Lynch, Brendan

Tunes from the Hearth, 'own label' BLCD01.

McCann, Brenda

Inishkeeragh, own label BMCD 02.

McCarthy, Johnny

The Square Triangle (with Con Ó Drisceoil and Pat Ahern), Craft Recordings CRCD02.

Mac Diarmada, Oisín

Traditional Music on Fiddle, Banjo & Harp (with Brian Fitzgerald and Micheál Ó Ruanaigh), Cló Iar-Chonnachta CICD 142.

McEvoy, John

Returning, Chart Music CHCD 057.

Mac Gabhann, Antóin

Ar Aon Bhuille – Matching Beats, Cló Iar-Chonnachta CICD 105.

McGann, Andy

It's a Hard Road to Travel (with Paul Brady), Shanachie 34011.
The Funny Reel (with Joe Burke and Felix Dolan), Shanachie 34016.

McGann, Andy, and Paddy Reynolds

Andy McGann and Paddy Reynolds, Shanachie 34008.

McGlinchey, Brendan

Music of a Champion, Silverhill PSH 100.

McGreevy, Johnny

The Noonday Feast (with Joe Shannon), Green Linnet CSIF 1023.
Johnny McGreevy and Séamus Cooley, Cló Iar-Chonnachta CIC 021.

McGuire, Manus

Saffron and Blue, Green Linnet GLCD 1206.

McGuire, Séamus

An Ríl ar Lár - The Missing Reel (with John Lee), Gael-Linn CEFCD 146.
The Wishing Tree, Green Linnet GLCD 1151.

McGuire, Séamus and Manus

The Humours of Lissadell, Folk Legacy FSE 78.
Carousel (with Daithí Sproule), Gael-Linn CEFCD 105.
Buttons and Bows (with Jackie Daly), Green Linnet GLCD 1051.
The First Month of Summer, Green Linnet GLCD 1079.

McGuire, Seán

Seán Maguire Plays, Viva VV 103.
At His Best (with Roger Sherlock and Josephine Keegan) Outlet PTICD 1002.
Champion of Champions (with Josephine Keegan), Outlet PTICD 1005.
Traditional Irish Fiddle (with Josephine Keegan), Outlet PTICD 1006.
The Very Best of (with Roger Sherlock and Josephine Keegan), Outlet PTICD 1008.
Two Champions (with Joe Burke), Outlet PTICD 1014.
Ireland's Champion Fiddler, Outlet PTICD 3031.

Man of Achievement (with Josephine Keegan), Outlet PTICD 1052.

From the Archives, Outlet OAS 3017.

Portráid, Gael-Linn CEFC 137.

Sixty Years of Irish Fiddle, Celtic Music CM 043.

Hawks and Doves of Irish Culture, Outlet PTICD 1089.

The Master's Touch, Ainm Records ARCD 027.

McGuire, Seán and Jim

Brothers Together, Outlet PTICD 1055.

McKillop, Jim

Irish Traditional Fiddle Music, Outlet PTICD 1045.

McNamara, Seán, and Éamon Coyne

The Long Strand – Irish Fiddle Music from Liverpool, VeteranTapes VT 125.

Meehan, Danny

Navvy on the Shore, Bow Hand 001CD.

Milne, Vince

A Small Island – Traditional Music from Cork (with Pat Sullivan and Bríd Cranitch), Ossian OSSCD 70.

Morrison, James

James Morrison and Tom Ennis, Topic 12T390.

The Pure Genius of James Morrison, Shanachie 33004.

The Professor, Viva Voce 001 (2 cassettes).

Mulvihill, Brendan

The Flax in Bloom, Green Linnet GLCD 1020.

The Morning Dew, Green Linnet GLCD 1128.

Mulvihill, Martin

Traditional Irish Fiddling from County Limerick, Green Linnet CSIF 1012.

Murphy, Denis

Music from Sliabh Luachra, Radio Telefís Éireann RTECD 183.

Murphy, Denis, and Julia Clifford

The Star Above the Garter, Claddagh CC5CD.

Murphy, Peter

The Dawn, Music Box MBMC 1022.

Neff, Eoghan

Soundpost and Bridle (with Flaithrí Neff), Teaghlach T001.

Ní Mhaonaigh, Máiréad

Ceol Aduaidh (with Frankie Kennedy), Gael-Linn CEFCD 102.

Altan (with Frankie Kennedy), Green Linnet GLCD 1078.

O'Brien, Eileen

Newtown Bridge, Moanfin Recordings CD001.

O'Connell, Connie

Ceol go Maidin (with Jimmy Doyle and Séamus Mac Mathúna), Comhaltas CL 43.

Ceol Chill na Martra, Shanachie 78033.

O'Connor, Gerry

Cosa Gan Bhróga (with Eithne Ní Uallacháin and Dessie Wilkinson), Gael-Linn CEFC 111.

Lá Lugh (with Eithne Ní Uallacháin), Claddagh CCF29CD.

Brighid's Kiss (with Eithne Ní Uallacháin), Lughnasa Music LUGCD 961.

O'Connor, Kevin

From the Chest, Malgamú Music MALGCD113.

O'Donnell, Eugene

Slow Airs and Set Dances (with Mick Moloney), Green Linnet GLCD1015.

The Foggy Dew (with James McCafferty), Green Linnet GLCD1084.

O'Keeffe, Máire

Cóisir - House Party, Gael-Linn CEFCD 165.

O'Keeffe, Pádraig

The Sliabh Luachra Fiddle Master, Radio Telefís Éireann RTECD 174.

O'Keeffe, Pádraig, Denis Murphy and Julia Clifford

Kerry Fiddles - Fiddle Music from Sliabh Luachra, Topic 12T309; Ossian OSSCD 10.

O'Leary, Dan

Traditional Music from the Kingdom of Kerry (with Jimmy Doyle), Shanachie 29007.

O'Loughlin, Peter

Traditional Music from County Clare (with Ronan Browne), Claddagh CC47.

Ó Raghallaigh, Caoimhín

Turas go Tír na nÓg, own label no number.

O'Shaughnessy, Paul

Within a Mile of Dublin (with Paul McGrattan), Foetain SPINCD1000.

Stay Another While (with Frankie Lane), own label POSCD0001.

Peoples, Tommy

Tommy Peoples, Comhaltas CL 13.

The High Part of the Road (with Paul Brady), Shanachie 34007.

Matt Molloy, Tommy Peoples, Paul Brady, Mulligan LUNCD 017; Green Linnet GLCD 3018.

The Iron Man (with Daithí Sproule), Shanachie 79044.

Traditional Irish Music Played on the Fiddle, GTD Heritage TRAD HCD 008.

Master Irish Fiddle Player, Ovation OVA 503.

The Quiet Glen, own label TPCD001.

Potts, Tommy

The Liffey Banks, Claddagh CC13CD.

Power, Jimmy

Irish Fiddle Player, Topic 12TS306; Ossian OSS 81.

Queally, Michael

The Trip over the Mountain, own label QOD001.

Rooney, Brian

The Godfather, Racket Records RRCD002.

Ryan, Joe

Crossroads (with Eddie Clarke), Green Linnet CSIF 1030.

An Buachaill Dreoite, Cló Iar-Chonnachta CICD 113.

Two Gentlemen of Clare Music (with Gerard Commane), Clachán Music CMCD001.

Smyth, Seán

The Blue Fiddle, Mulligan LUNCD 060.

Vesey, John

The First Month of Spring, Shanachie 29006.

Sligo Fiddle, own label no number (double CD).

The following recordings are compilations featuring the playing of those listed.

An Fhidil: 1, Gael-Linn CEF 068,

Séamus Glackin, Martin Hayes, Maurice Lennon, Seán Montgomery, Séamus Thompson.

An Fhidil: 2, Gael-Linn CEF 069,

Kevin Burke, Séamus Creagh, Paddy Glackin, Seán Keane.

Ceol an Chláir 1, Comhaltas CL 17,

Bobby Casey, Junior Crehan, John Kelly, Patrick Kelly, Joe Ryan.

Dear Old Erin's Isle – Irish Traditional Music from America, Nimbus NI 5350,

(Recorded live at the annual *Éigse na Laoi* Festival, University College Cork, February 1992),

Liz Carroll, Kevin Burke, Séamus Connolly, Brendan Mulvihill, Eileen Ivers, (with Séamus Egan, Tom Doherty, John Williams, Jimmy Keane, Joe Shannon, Billy McComiskey).

Fiddle Fair, own label no number,

(Recorded live at the annual *Fiddle Fair* at Declan McCarthy's, Baltimore, Co. Cork, May 2000),

Dezi Donnelly, Cathal Hayden, Matt Cranitch, Dermot McLaughlin, Liz Doherty, Sheila Garry, Liz Kane, Nollaig Casey, Yvonne Kane, (with Michael McGoldrick, Éamonn McElholm, Brian McGrath, Mick Daly, Dave Hennessy, Paul McGrattan, Ian Carr, Noel Ryan, Arty McGlynn, Russel's House, At the Racket).

Fiddlesticks – Irish Traditional Music from Donegal, Nimbus NI 5320,

(Recorded live at the annual *Éigse na Laoi* Festival, University College Cork, January 1991),

Ciarán Tourish, Dermot McLaughlin, Séamus Glackin, Kevin Glackin, Tommy Peoples, Séamus Gibson, Proinsias Ó Maonaigh, Máiréad Ní Mhaonaigh, Paula Doohan, Liz Doherty.

Milestone at the Garden – Irish Fiddle Masters from the 78 RPM Era, Rounder Records CD1123,

James Morrison, John Howard, Fireman Barney Conlon, Frank Quinn, Paddy Cronin, Hugh Gillespie, Denis Murphy, Frank O'Higgins, Paddy Killoran, K. Scanlon, Danny O'Donnell, Francis Cashin, Tom Cawley, Seán Ryan, Loius E. Quinn, James O'Beirne, Michael Coleman, Neil O'Boyle, Seán Maguire, Kathleen Harrington, Michael Hanafin, Ed Reavy, Paddy Canny, Packie Dolan, Patrick Sweeney.

My Love is in America, Green Linnet GLCD 1110,
  (Recorded live at *The Boston College Irish Fiddle Festival*, March 1990),
  Kevin Burke, Liz Carroll, Séamus Connolly, Brian Conway, Johnny Cronin,
  Paddy Cronin, Tony DeMarco, Martin Hayes, Eileen Ivers, James Kelly, Andy
  McGann, Johnny McGreevy, Brendan Mulvihill, Paddy Reynolds, Dale Russ,
  Martin Wynne, (with Mel Mercier).

Playing With Fire - The Celtic Fiddle Collection, Green Linnet GLCD 1101,
  Kevin Burke, Liz Carroll, Séamus Connolly, Brian Conway, Johnny
  Cunningham, Tony DeMarco, Maeve Donnelly, Eileen Ivers, Seán Keane,
  Christian Lemaitre, Séamus and Manus Maguire, Brendan Mulvihill, Máiréad
  Ní Mhaonaigh, Eugene O'Donnell, Paul O'Shaughnessy.

The Brass Fiddle – Traditional Irish Music from Donegal, Claddagh CC44CD,
  Francie Byrne, James Byrne, Vincent Campbell, Con Cassidy.

The Donegal Fiddle. Radio Telefís Éireann RTECD 196,
  Francie Dearg O Beirn, Mickey Bán O Beirn, Mickey Simi Doherty, John
  Gallagher, James Josie McHugh, Paddy Gallagher, Jimmy Lyons, John Simi
  Doherty, Simon Simi Doherty.

The Fiddle Music of Donegal: Vol. 1, Cáirdeas Recordings CNF001,
  Martin McGinley, Jimmy Campbell, Michael McMenamin, Mick Brown,
  Proinnsias Ó Maonaigh, Danny McCarry, Peter Tracey, Paul O'Shaughnessy.

The Fiddle Music of Donegal: Vol. 2, Cáirdeas Recordings CNF002,
  Vincent Campbell, Maurice Bradley, Stephen Campbell, Róisín McGrory,
  Damien Harrigan, James Byrne, Ronan Galvin.

The Fiddle Music of Donegal: Vol. 3, Cáirdeas Recordings CNF003,
  Dermot McLaughlin, John Byrne, Derek McGinley, Matthew McGranaghan,
  Jimmy Campbell, Peter Campbell.

The Music of Ed Reavy, Rounder 6008; Ossian OSS 49; Cló Iar-Chonnachta CIC 047,
  Liz Carroll, Maeve Donnelly, Martin Mulvihill, Tony DeMarco, Ed Reavy,
  Armin Barnett, Brendan Mulvihill, Maureen Fitzpatrick, Eugene O'Donnell,
  Paddy Cronin, Louis Quinn, (with Mick Moloney, Billy McComiskey, Andy
  O'Brien, Shelly Posen, Tim Britton, Larry McCullough, Eugene Curry).

Index of Tunes

POLKAS

REELS

HORNPIPES

SET DANCES

AIRS

Johnnie McFadden and Jeannie McAllister of Co. Antrim
Photograph courtesy of Comhaltas Ceoltóirí Éireann

for further information about Ossian's range of Irish music in book, audio and DVD formats contact us at:

Ossian Publications Ltd. Music Sales Ltd, Newmarket Road, Bury St Edmunds, Suffolk, IP33 3YB, Great Britain

O S S I A N

CD TRACK LISTING

In order to demonstrate the particular points being made in each case, the examples are generally played slower tha[n] normal. On tracks 7, 8, 25 and 26, they are played at two tempos, slowly first and then faster. On each of tracks 20 an[d] 35, two tunes are played together to comprise a set of tunes as would usually be done by traditional musicians. Pian[o] accompaniment is provided by Bríd Cranitch on tracks 36, 37, 42, 51 and 52. To hear less of the piano, the stereo balanc[e] control should be turned to the right.

No. Track Title

1. Notes of the open strings: A, D, G, E
2. *The Connachtman's Rambles*
3. The 'Cut'
4. The 'Double Cut'
5. *The Connachtman's Rambles*
6. *The Hag's Purse*
7. The 'Roll'
8. *The Rambling Pitchfork*
9. *The Rose in the Heather*
10. *The High Part of the Road*
11. *Give us a Drink of Water*
12. *Mick Duggan's Slide*
13. *Denis Murphy's Slide (1)*
14. *The Brosna Slide*
15. *The Scartaglen Slide*
16. *The Top of Maol*
17. *Seán McGovern's Polka*
18. *Dálaigh's Polka*
19. *The Lakes of Sligo*
20. *The Top of Maol & The Scartaglen Polka*
21. *The Boys of Bluehill*
22. *Cronin's Hornpipe*
23. *The Kildare Fancy*
24. *Rodney's Glory*
25. *Anything for John Joe?*
26. *The Peeler's Jacket*
27. *Jackie Coleman's Reel*
28. *The Humours of Tulla*
29. *The Woman of the House*
30. *The Humours of Carrigaholt*
31. *The Moving Bog*
32. *The Man of the House*
33. *The Piper's Despair*
34. *The Old Pigeon on the Gate*
35. *The Pretty Girls of Mayo & Rolling on the Ryegrass*
36. *Sheebeg and Sheemore*
37. *Carolan's Draught*
38. *Cáit Ní Dhuibhir*
39. *Amhrán na Leabhar*
40. *An Goirtín Eornan*
41. *Aisling Gheal*
42. *Sliabh na mBan*
43. *The Wheels of the Worl[d]*
44. *O'Callaghan's Hornpip[e]*
45. *Miss Langford*
46. *The Red-Haired Lass*
47. *Caoineadh an Spailpín*
48. *Denis Murphy's Slide (*
49. *The Dark Girl*
50. *The Cliffs of Moher*
51. *Doctor Gilbert*
52. *Lucy Campbell*

To remove your CD from the plastic sleeve, lift the small lip to break the perforations. Replace the disc after use for convenient storage.

Printed in the EU 1/07 (6093